The Brown
UNIVERSITY BAND

The Brown
UNIVERSITY BAND
An Ever True History

SEAN BRIODY

THE
History
PRESS

Published by The History Press
Charleston, SC
www.historypress.com

First published 2024

Manufactured in the United States

ISBN 9781467154437

Library of Congress Control Number: 2023947098

Notice: The information in this book is true and complete to the best of our knowledge. It is offered without guarantee on the part of the author or The History Press. The author and The History Press disclaim all liability in connection with the use of this book.

For all those who don't just settle for being a part of something but want to go that extra step and find out why.

CONTENTS

FOREWORD

*T*he extraordinarily unique passion and enthusiasm that the Brown University Band brings to an event is familiar to any Brunonian, and there has always been a special connection between the band and the Bears' athletics teams.

From my days as a student-athlete in the early 1990s to my current tenure leading our division, I have been fortunate to be a part of so many memorable moments that were made that much better by the irreplaceable presence of the band. I know that feeling is shared by generations of Brown students, as the band has worked tirelessly to enhance events in all corners of our campus.

We remain grateful for the excitement, energy and spirit that the Brown University Band brings to life on College Hill, and we are delighted that Sean Briody has chosen to so eloquently tell their story.

—M. Grace Calhoun '92, PhD
The Chancellor Samuel M. Mencoff '78 Vice President
for Athletics and Recreation
Brown University

ACKNOWLEDGEMENTS

*W*hen I joined the Brown Band in the fall of 2015, I was just a kid who wanted to bang drums. In fact, I was especially jealous of multiple friends and future roommates, whose skills were far superior to mine. However, I soon felt the sense of community that the band possesses, be it a quirky tradition or the table of band members that is seemingly always full in the dining hall. As I progressed through Brown, I realized the importance of the band as a student organization. Having always possessed a love of history, I became more and more curious about the band's story and discovered there wasn't much of a written record anywhere. I eventually made the band my thesis topic, written for an honors degree in American Studies.

In my thesis, I focused on the traditions of the band as a student organization, which are vital to its continuous operation. However, along the way, I found many interesting historical stories that I wanted to include but did not because they were irrelevant to my argument. And thus, here we are with this book, something I never dreamed I could write. It is by no means perfect. However, it is certainly a good start, considering no large-scale history of the band has ever been composed.[1]

Throughout the project, I interviewed or corresponded with multiple Brown alumni and personnel whose contributions were vital to the completion of my work, including:

Yeshaya Douglas Ballon

Bill Barnert

Ken Blackman

William Brakewood

Dennis Ciccarillo

Zoe Fieldsteel

Farrell Fleming

Charles Gagnon

Hilary Gerstein

Susan Gilmore

Zachary Goldstein

Bill Hochheiser

Rich Hofmann

Ulysses James

David Josephson

Isabela Karibjanian

Lauren Kupersmith

Irving Lustig

Matthew McGarrell

Karen Mellor

Michael O'Brien

Paul Payton

Tucker Peck

Rosie Perera

Vicky Phan

Becky Sheinbaum

Kenneth Sloan

Marvin Wasser

Michael Weston

Lisa Yanek

Dan Zemel

Harry Zisson

Doug Hackett, Richard Levy and Jane Strauss Holzkamp provided important archival material to support my search for information. Furthermore, Professor Robert P. Emlen was a phenomenal thesis advisor, and Professor Steven D. Lubar provided excellent insight as a second reader. This also could not have been written without the assistance of Raymond Butti Jr., Jennifer Betts and Paul Jordan of the John Hay Library University Archives, who paged hundreds of boxes of material for me over the years, as well as the support of University Librarian Joseph Meisel. Dr. Joseph Pucci, Zachary Goldstein, Gus Kmetz, Kellan Barr and countless others provided strong encouragement in the project. In its original form, Jacob Ihnen and Tobias Berggruen made much-needed suggestions, in terms of both grammar and content. In addition to his constant support, near the completion of the book, Daniel Erdosy very generously drove out to Taunton, Massachusetts, to pick up the original snare drum photographed in the text. I also wish to recognize Kate Wells of the Providence Public Library for paging and scanning photographs of D.W. Reeves, as well as Becca Bender of the Rhode Island Historical Society for digitizing two archival films of the band that helped my research.

I am also indebted to my parents, Stephen and Mary Briody, who listened to me drone on and on about the history of the band for years and finally encouraged me to put all of my thoughts on paper. Without them, this wouldn't exist.

And finally, to my students at Cardinal Newman School, who, when they heard of my book's publication, promised they would buy multiple copies.

"

INTRODUCTION

Student conductor Malachi Hornbuckle '22 poses with the Quinnipiac bobcat. *Brown University Band.*

"*E*ver True." These two words title Brown's main fight song and are overused, be it in emails or in book titles. I struggled for months as to whether or not I should use them to title this work, seeing as there are already histories of Brown crew and football and a tribute to Art Joukowsky that share that title.

However, regardless of the title, as I sit down to write this introduction, I realize that there is no organization so emblematic of loyalty—so fitting of the moniker "Ever True"—as the Brown University Band. Through rain, sleet, snow and even nor'easter, for one hundred years the Brown Band has traveled all over the country to support its student athletes. The band members represent the spirit of Brown and consider themselves the keepers of its traditions. At Campus Dance, only the band members know the words to the "Alma Mater" when it is sung on the steps of Sayles Hall, and they are usually the ones whose voices stand out from the crowd as they belt the words at the top of their lungs. Therefore, I find it wholly appropriate, for I know this devotion will continue.

You don't need to be a Brown alumnus to enjoy this work. I've sought to tell the story of this organization through a number of entertaining anecdotes. After a brief history of early music at Brown and the story of the band's founding, you'll find yourself immersed in a whimsical history, and I do hope you'll enjoy it.

Chapter 1

GROWTH OF THE "SINGING COLLEGE"

A HISTORY OF MUSIC AND SONGS AT BROWN

*T*he Brown University Band claims its founding date as 1924. However, to begin a history at that time would ignore the early roots of music at Brown and the reasons for the establishment of the present band. Small bands and orchestras at Brown are known to have existed in the early and mid-nineteenth century, but they never endured the test of time as permanent student groups.[2] Written evidence notes small musical performances at early nineteenth-century commencements and junior and senior exhibitions.

For decades in the nineteenth and twentieth centuries, the Brown University Glee, Banjo and Mandolin Clubs supplied the Brown and Providence communities with musical enjoyment and also went on a number of tours.

One nineteenth-century alumnus recalled:

> *The Brown musical clubs followed the pattern that was common at American College in the 90s. There was a glee club with membership of about 16; a mandolin club with mandolins and guitars, about 10 in all, to which we added later a violin or a cello, or a flute, or a combination of these; and a banjo club with banjos, banjeaurines (a short banjo with a big head), guitars and later a piccolo banjo. There was a great deal of overlapping in the membership and the three clubs formed one organization with a common manager. We made extended trips during Christmas and Easter vacations, and also gave a number of concerts in or near Providence....For each performance we received either a flat sum or a fraction of the gate receipts. I*

RAH-RAH ! RAH-RAH ! RAH-RAH ! BROWN !

FIFTH ANNUAL SUMMER TOUR
OF THE
Brown University Quartette, Banjo and Mandolin Clubs.

Engraved and Printed by Lux Eng. Co., Boston.

G. H. EISWALD. W. S. HAWKINS. E. W. JOHNSON. C. M. GALLUP. JOSEPH WALTHER. S. A. HOPKINS.
ARTHUR LLEWELLYN. J. O. OTIS. W. P. OTIS. C. S. ALDRICH.
L. H. NEWHELL. E. S. ROBERTS. A. C. STONE.

A booklet advertising a summer tour of the Brown Musical Clubs, 1893. *Author's private collection.*

don't think we ever failed to come out in the black at the end of the season,
and the profit was divided among the members of the club.[3]

The earliest organized band at Brown was the Brown Brass Band, founded
in 1889 and led by Arthur Hutchins Colby, class of 1891.[4] The group was
student-organized, with its first rehearsals held in Colby's dormitory Slater
Hall, and it performed at Brown football and baseball games.[5] A likely cause
for its formation was the long-standing success of Brown's Glee Club and
Symphony Society. Early members included future Brown chancellor Henry
Dexter Sharpe and his brother Lucian Sharpe. Their legacies live on in the
Sharpe Refectory, Brown's main dining hall. The Brown Brass Band practiced
military-style marching, though it was found to have recruiting issues during
the 1890s, as Brown men did not always play the required instruments.[6] Its
last appearance was in 1900, with articles in the years following lamenting
its loss and requesting its reinstatement.[7] It restarted in 1906 and lasted for a

short time before disappearing from mention altogether. A new Brown Band formed in the 1916–17 school year under D. Steele '16 and sporadically appeared at games for the next few years under different leaders, most notably Captain John W. Haley. At that time, the band was likely connected to the large military presence on campus during World War I.[8]

While Brown may have lacked a consistent student band, it most certainly had its fair share of school songs; by the early twentieth century, Brown was known as the "singing college." In fact, Colby was a co-compiler of the first university songbook, *Songs of Brown University* (1891). Most of the songs in Colby's book have become distant memories (including, thankfully, the works composed for the Brown University Minstrels), but four remain: "Alma Mater," "On the Chapel Steps," "Here's to Good Old Brown" and the Brown Commencement March. The oldest school song is Brown's "Alma Mater," written by Dr. James Andrews DeWolf in 1860. Originally called "Old Brown," as four of the verses contain references to "Old Brown" or "Brunonia" (DeWolf himself actually preferred this title), the song first appeared in the *Brown Paper* and was rediscovered and performed by the Brown Glee Club in June 1869. DeWolf graduated from Brown in 1861 and

Brown Brass Band, 1889. *Brown University Archives.*

Former members of the Brown Brass Band pose with members of the current Brown Band, 1929. *Brown University Archives.*

joined the Union army as a private, became an "acting assistant surgeon" and then earned his medical degree from Columbia in 1865.[9] After practicing in Providence for a few years, DeWolf relocated to Trinidad in 1870 when he was appointed surgeon general of the British Colonial Medical Service.[10] As the song was unpopular upon its composition, DeWolf was shocked years later to receive a newspaper clipping in the mail from his father about a Brown Glee Club concert where his piece was the finale! It is sung to the tune of "Araby's Daughter," perhaps better recognized as "The Old Oaken Bucket." As part of a tradition dating to the late nineteenth century, the "Alma Mater" is proudly sung by members of the graduating class on the steps of Sayles Hall during commencement weekend, though it should be noted that usually only members of the Brown Band know the words by memory. To the band, the "Alma Mater" is the most cherished Brown song

and is only played should the Bears win. Band members put their arms around one another and sway while singing the first few lines of the first verse before playing the rest. According to tradition, it is bad luck to say "Alma Mater" before or during a game, for that dooms Brown to lose. Thus, the band refers to it as "Apple Mango," "That Song," "A Llama Matters" or something similar. If someone does let it slip out, the band makes sure to point at them and chant, "It's all your fault!"

> *I need not say that it has been very gratifying to me that the verses in which I endeavored to express the sentiments animating the loyal sons of Brown in 1860–61 have been appreciated and deemed worthy of adoption by their successors, and it is pleasant to think that the "offering of praise" long ago laid upon the altar of Alma Mater is still daily renewed by her no less loyal sons of a later day.*
> —*J.A. DeWolf* [11]

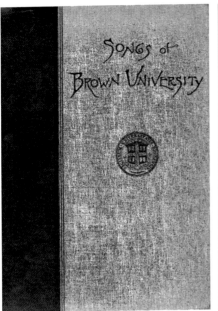 

Left: *Songs of Brown University* (1891). *Author's private collection.*

Right: James Andrews DeWolf, 1861. *Brown University Archives.*

DeWolf died on January 2, 1909, in Port of Spain, Trinidad, but his musical legacy lives on.[12] One classmate of his wrote, "There can be no more pathetic scene when that at 'last prayers' of the year, when the graduating class, all standing and many tearful, chant the loved and familiar verses. It is to our college what the 'Star Spangled Banner' is to the Army and Navy.... Surely, we should have his [DeWolf's] portrait...among our noted graduates and friends in Sayles Hall."[13]

Another early vocal work was "On the Chapel Steps." Described as "a genuine college song with real college atmosphere and beauty," this piece has a unique history, as it was composed by two Brown students and soon became a common college song at other campuses.[14] The music was composed by George Coleman Gow (class of 1884), while Joel Nelson Eno (class of 1883) wrote the words. Gow and Eno wrote the song while members of Delta Epsilon fraternity at Brown, a group that helped popularize it in the 1880s. Gow was a music professor at Vassar College for decades, while Eno became a writer and historian.[15] Though not often played by the Brown Band, this piece is usually performed on solemn occasions such as vigils and is more commonly performed by the vocal groups on campus.

The traditional "Here's to Good Old Brown" is a tune that can be found throughout American college songbooks. However, the chorus of the song was abandoned in the late twentieth century; now, when the Brown Band performs this song, it plays the introductory "Here's to good old Brown, drink her down, drink her down..." and then segues into "I'm a Brown Man Born," an adaptation of the University of North Carolina's "I'm a Tarheel Born," which was "stolen" by the Brown baseball team after a 1903 game.[16]

Like "Brown Man Born," some other Brown University songs were adapted from other universities. John B. Archer (1872–1954) was a Providence composer and arranger. He directed the Brown University Musical Clubs for a short time, as well as the University Glee Club of Providence, the Choral Art Society and the Providence Festival Chorus.[17] In 1921, Thomas Appleget and W.T. Hastings edited a new version of *Songs of Brown University*; Archer was the vocal arranger for the pieces included in this new edition. Before that, Archer composed the polka "Brown Bear," an adaptation of a piece originally written by O. Kenneth Quivey for Purdue University under the title "Let's Go Purdue."[18] He later became university organist.

Brown's unique Commencement March was likely composed in the early nineteenth century, though its composer is "T. Brown," likely a pseudonym.[19] David Wallis Reeves, leader of Providence's American Band, arranged the piece into its current form.[20] Supposedly an original copy of the march, containing a never-before-heard coda described as "the most brilliant part of the composition," belonged to American Band cornetist Bowen R. Church but is now lost.[21] The American Band performed at Brown's commencement ceremony as far back as 1847 and seems to have performed the march itself at commencement beginning at least in 1869, until being superseded by the Brown Band in 1970.[22]

> [J]ust in advance of the procession marched Reeves' American Band.... Then the March was played not as it sometimes is today, with a heavy thumping of drums and a small trickle of music, but quite the reverse. The drums seemed muted, and the brass instruments blared forth in all their might. They fairly took you off your feet, and their playing, to the children at least, was the high spot in a gala day.[23]

The Commencement March is unique to Brown, and one story relates that Reeves attempted to play it at Dartmouth, only to have the band break down and stop playing as it did not feel appropriate.[24] In 1909, Thatcher H. Guild wrote "Brown Men All," a musically similar piece that was meant to

Left: David Wallis Reeves portrait, circa 1900. *David Wallis Reeves's American Band Collection, Providence Public Library, Providence, Rhode Island.*

Below: Matthew McGarrell instructs the band prior to commencement, March 2017. *Brown University Band.*

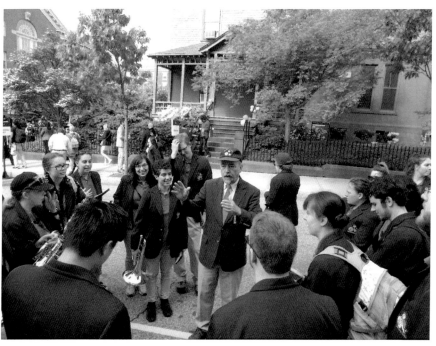

be an introduction to the Commencement March; despite its inclusion in the 1921 Brown songbook, this piece did not remain in memory for long.[25] The Brown Band continues to perform the Commencement March today, using an arrangement created by advisor Matthew McGarrell.

Many of Brown's fight songs were composed in the first decade of the twentieth century. Brown's main fight song, "Ever True to Brown," made its first appearance in November 1905. It was composed by a freshman, Donald Jackson, class of 1909.[26] Born in Barrington, Rhode Island, in 1886, Jackson was a frequent composer of school melodies. He was a member of the Brown Musical Clubs and directed the Providence Symphony Orchestra shortly after his graduation. Among the other notable pieces still played by the band that he composed are "For Bruno and for Brown" (1912)[27] and "Bring the Victory to Brown" (1919).[28] However, "Ever True" is by far the most well known of them, having now become Brown's official fight song, though it was not initially this popular. A harsh 1926 *Brown Daily Herald* called it "probably the worst of all Brown songs" but yet "the only tune to which all of us know the words."[29] Jackson remained active in Brown alumni groups and even won an alumni songwriting competition with his "Glory of Old Brown" (1948).[30]

Another winner of the aforementioned songwriting contest was Fred A. Otis (class of 1903) with his "Brown Forevermore."[31] Otis was also a member of the Brown Musical Clubs as an undergraduate but never composed for the college repertoire as a student. However, unlike Jackson's winning entry, Otis's song remains in the band's repertoire, performed on the march to the football stadium. Additionally, "Brunonia's Big Brown Team," later renamed "The Brown Cheering Song," was composed by Robert Bradford Jones, class of 1907, and Howard S. Young, class of 1908, and with the prior two compositions has cemented itself in the Brown Band's main repertoire.

During hockey season, the band plays "Ki-Yi-Yi," composed by Edward Warren Corliss and William A. Hart (class of 1903). Corliss was a member of the class of 1895 but did not graduate. He had a semi-successful career as a composer of operettas but died prematurely in September 1916 at the age of forty-four.[32] The song's title alludes to the sound a wounded animal makes in the wild.

Another notable composer of Brown songs was Alfred Griswold Chaffee, class of 1902. Chaffee (1882–1961) grew up in East Providence, described as a "boy wonder" after he once played a concert with Reeves's American Band.[33] He composed "Brunonia (As We Go Marching)"; "Bruno," a favorite of the band for the first thirty years of its existence that has unexpectedly left

"Ki-Yi-Yi" sheet music. *Brown University Archives.*

the band's repertoire; and "In the Fray," which is played by the band during each of its ice shows.

A description of Brown University songs would not be complete without mentioning the songs of Pembroke College, Brown University's women's college that was founded in 1891. Pembroke students adopted many of the Brown songs and adapted a number of them to reflect its female population. The glee club of the women's college put out a number of songbooks in the early part of the twentieth century; a quick review of them shows Pembroke-specific titles like "The Brown Bred Girl" and "Hail to Our Own Dean King." However, a number of familiar songs are printed, such as the Commencement March, "Alma Mater" and "Oh Mother Dear Brunonia."[34]

All of these songs play an important part in the traditions carried on by the Brown University Band. No official university songbook has been published since 1928; however, while Brown may no longer be the "singing college," the songs do not disappear from history, as the band continues to keep them alive. All of this leads to an underlying argument that is found throughout this book: the members of the Brown University Band are the keepers of tradition at Brown. As the unofficial keepers of Brown traditions and customs, band members often grimace when they hear someone incorrectly telling the story behind the Ratty or the Rock on a campus tour. The band also lays claim to its own set of traditions; not necessarily knowing *why* they do certain things the way they do, band members just know that they sing a "bus driver cheer" upon arriving back at Fulton Rehearsal Hall from a long away trip, sing "O, Canada" at I-95 rest stops and yell a vulgar cheer while approaching a tollbooth because that is how it has traditionally been done. Stories of the band's traditions will be found interweaved throughout this work, as the history of the band is told chronologically. Both the band's traditions and its history are vital to understanding its importance to the Brown community today.

The next chapter details the founding of the present-day band as can be best gleaned from existing documentation. It should be noted that varying accounts of the band's founding exist, one by Irving Harris and two by Joseph Strauss, both of which appear to omit details when juxtaposed with the *Brown Daily Herald* and scrapbooks maintained by Harris. Hopefully, what follows will help clarify the historical record.

Chapter 2

A MOP HANDLE AND A BATHROBE CORD

THE BEGINNINGS OF THE BROWN BAND

*T*he story of the Brown University Band begins with a young man born in New York City on November 4, 1906. Irving Harcourt Harris, the son of textile manufacturer Abraham Harris and his wife, Rose, graduated from the Peddie School in Hightstown, New Jersey, and entered Brown University alongside his Peddie roommate Joseph Strauss, whose own role in the band's founding should not be underestimated.

After arriving on campus in the fall of 1924, Harris was determined to be involved in Brown's musical clubs in some way. Thus, he auditioned for Brown's orchestra with his piccolo, but alas, he was not admitted.[35] Following his failed audition, Harris sat in the football stands on October 4, 1924, watching the Brown men play against Colby College. He turned to a sophomore acquaintance and asked when the Brown Marching Band would put in an appearance. Having heard of the stellar marching bands at schools like Yale, Harvard and Princeton, Harris expected to join Brown's group and wished to introduce himself to its leader. Much to Harris's surprise, he was told that such a band did not exist; at least, not in the way that he expected it to. An informal band was led by Philip Grossman Bronstein '26, who had founded it the previous year.[36] It consisted of twenty-five members, with Bronstein optimistic that it would grow to thirty-five for the coming football season.[37] Bronstein had placed notices in the *Brown Daily Herald* the week before the Colby game and assembled a rehearsal on that Friday night. His expectation was that the band would be ready by the following week; he had no plans to appear at the contest against Colby.[38] It was decisions like this that led Harris to later deem Bronstein's band a "dismal failure."[39]

Irving Harcourt Harris '28, founder of the Brown University Band. *Brown University Band.*

Harris became worked up over the absence of a steady, reliable band and turned to his aforementioned roommate, Joseph Loeb Strauss Jr., of Chicago, for guidance. Strauss had heard of the football team's upcoming game in Chicago the following weekend and knew that the next Wednesday there would be a large sendoff parade to accompany the team to the train station. Motivated by the prospect of having the band out for the occasion, Strauss urged Harris to call a rehearsal for the band—in this case, a new band, separate from the one advertised as being led by Bronstein. Harris posted rehearsal notices around campus and was laughed at, for a freshman creating his own student organization was deemed impossible in those days. As a faculty member later recalled:

> *No [Brown] Freshman had ever before started an all-college organization; no Freshman had ever before faced University officials and members of the alumni for finances and no first-year man had ever before attempted to place upperclassmen under his own direction. What would have been extremely difficult for a member of the Senior class was believed to be nearly impossible for a Freshman.*[40]

After advertising a Monday night rehearsal, Harris and Strauss were in need of equipment. They scavenged across campus until they found a bass drum with a broken drumhead in the attic of Van Wickle Hall, left over from a small naval unit band that was stationed at Brown during World War I.[41] Nine men showed up that night, perhaps some enthusiastic freshmen, or perhaps some who were confused, thinking this was the Bronstein band. Nonetheless, Harris had their attention and led them in rehearsal with two marches he had bought earlier that morning, being sure to hide his freshman cap while doing so. The following night was a second rehearsal, this time with fourteen men in attendance.[42]

Despite this showing, Harris was hesitant to have the band out for the Chicago sendoff. Though the rehearsals had sounded musically promising, the band had never practiced marching. "And besides," Harris said to his roommate in an attempt to find a good excuse, "I have no drum major's stick."[43] Strauss's quick thinking, combined with a mop handle from the closet of Faunce House janitor Nelson "Nels" Lambert[44] and his own bathrobe cord, quickly solved that problem.[45] Additionally, Strauss pointed out that he had sent to the *Brown Daily Herald* a notice that the new "Big Brown Band" would appear to lead Wednesday's pre-game scrimmage rally at Andrews Field.[46] Thus, said Strauss, Harris had no choice. This notice

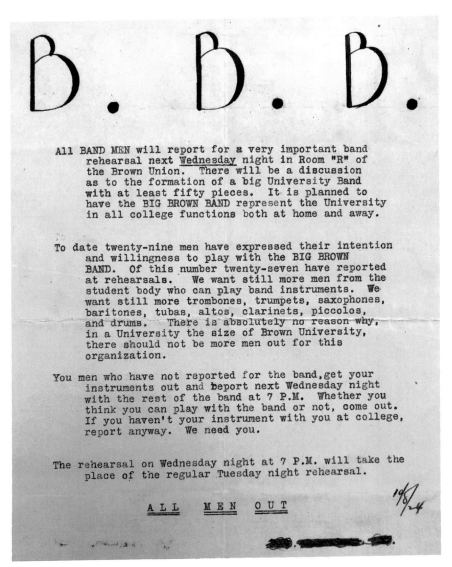

B. B. B.

All BAND MEN will report for a very important band rehearsal next <u>Wednesday</u> night in Room "R" of the Brown Union. There will be a discussion as to the formation of a big University Band with at least fifty pieces. It is planned to have the BIG BROWN BAND represent the University in all college functions both at home and away.

To date twenty-nine men have expressed their intention and willingness to play with the BIG BROWN BAND. Of this number twenty-seven have reported at rehearsals. We want still more men from the student body who can play band instruments. We want still more trombones, trumpets, saxophones, baritones, tubas, altos, clarinets, piccolos, and drums. There is absolutely no reason why, in a University the size of Brown University, there should not be more men out for this organization.

You men who have not reported for the band, get your instruments out and report next Wednesday night with the rest of the band at 7 P.M. Whether you think you can play with the band or not, come out. If you haven't your instrument with you at college, report anyway. We need you.

The rehearsal on Wednesday night at 7 P.M. will take the place of the regular Tuesday night rehearsal.

<u>A L L   M E N   O U T</u>

Above and opposite: Two of the notices that Harris and Strauss posted around campus to attract students, 1924. *Brown University Archives.*

was printed the next day, directly adjacent to an article about Manchester's band, which had rehearsed but remained undecided about its attendance.[47] The day before the sendoff parade, the band appeared at an Andrews Field rally with "a very creditable showing on its first appearance," with the *Herald* noting, "The music of the band helped enliven the rally and the students rid themselves of surplus steam with songs."[48]

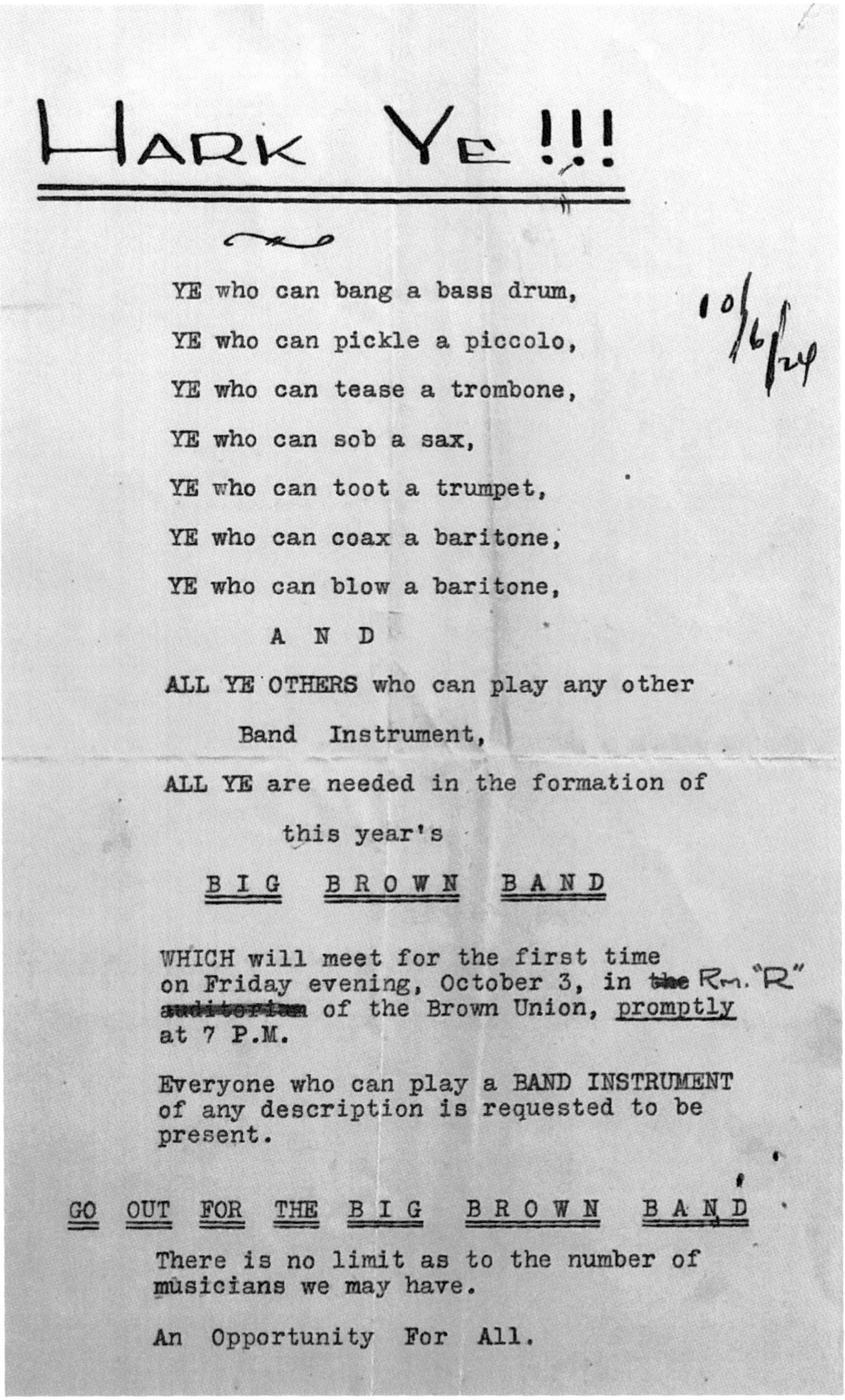

HARK YE !!!

YE who can bang a bass drum,

YE who can pickle a piccolo,

YE who can tease a trombone,

YE who can sob a sax,

YE who can toot a trumpet,

YE who can coax a baritone,

YE who can blow a baritone,

A N D

ALL YE OTHERS who can play any other

Band Instrument,

ALL YE are needed in the formation of

this year's

B I G   B R O W N   B A N D

WHICH will meet for the first time
on Friday evening, October 3, in ~~the~~ Rm. "R"
~~auditorium~~ of the Brown Union, promptly
at 7 P.M.

Everyone who can play a BAND INSTRUMENT
of any description is requested to be
present.

GO OUT FOR THE B I G   B R O W N   B A N D

There is no limit as to the number of
musicians we may have.

An Opportunity For All.

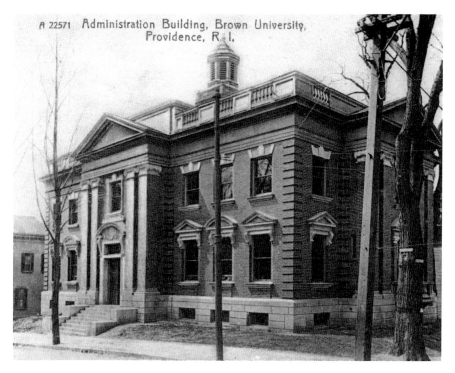

Van Wickle Hall (now demolished), where Harris and Strauss found surplus navy drums. *Brown University Archives.*

On Thursday morning, sixteen men showed up for the parade, those extra two perhaps being disappointed members of the other, absent band. The band lined up between Rockefeller Hall and Hope College and, with a traditional roll-off, began the march to the train station, cheerleaders and student body in tow. As Strauss recalled:

> *Almost the entire undergraduate body gathered on the Middle Campus after nine o'clock classes to cheer the departure of the team for Chicago. Led by cheerleaders stationed in the exact middle of the campus, cheer after cheer was given. Off in the area between Faunce House and Hope College gathered sixteen lonely musicians with no uniforms....Irving Harris equipped with the converted mop-stick lined them up nervously, four across, five deep, with a few vacancies in the rear ranks....Everyone was amazed to hear the timid beat of a drum and astonished to observe Brown's new band stepping off behind a leader whose only distinguishing mark was a Freshman cap turned inside out....For once, a Freshman led the parade.*[49]

Though its first performance was a triumphant moment in band history, in retrospect the sendoff was quite comical. The two songs that Harris had purchased and that the band played on the march were "Up the Street" and "Our Director," two *Harvard University* school songs![50] As a freshman, Harris had not yet explored Providence—and thus, he did not yet know the way to the station. Luckily, Providence policemen were directing traffic, so Harris found his way. The band's esteemed founder would also confess ten years later that he accidentally conducted the band through backward motions.[51]

So began the Brown University Band as it is today. Despite splashing on the scene the way it did, Harris's band had no funds with which to continue its operation. The university, in turn, pledged support to the band should it have promising attendance at the following week's Boston University game. After a successful showing, the *Herald* ran an article on November 10, noting that the Dartmouth Band was funded by alumni and students and that the Brown Band would need something similar in order to succeed.[52] Upon seeing this article, Dean of the College Otis Everett Randall invited Irving Harris to meet with him.[53] Two days later, on November 12, the band was officially reorganized with Harris as its new leader and conductor, Bronstein having given up all his written duties.[54] Randall urged students to join and support the band, especially in advance of the new football stadium opening in the fall of 1925.[55] Members were promised new uniforms and a year-end banquet in turn. When Harris was appointed leader, members were required to officially rejoin the new group, and men like Manchester and Bronstein permanently left the group.[56] Three days following the band's reorganization, Harris purchased an official drum major's baton, which he began to use for performances.[57]

The band practiced on Tuesday nights in the student union from 7:00 to 8:30 p.m. and played whether it had "five men or twenty."[58] Rehearsals were led by the band's first coach, Roswell H. Fairman, a former Spanish-American War musician who conducted the Providence Symphony Orchestra.[59] The group began rehearsing for the second semester at the end of February, following Harris's purchase of three marches and rental of two clarinets.[60] It made its first appearance of the year at Interclass

Week in March, playing at the basketball contest between the freshmen and sophomores, making "more than a creditable showing" and earning front-page praise from the Cammarian Club.[61]

The Brown baseball team was set to open the varsity baseball season at home against Connecticut State on April 18, and Harris knew the band needed to be present. In late March, Harris asked athletic director Fred W. Marvel if the band could have official uniforms. Without any hesitation, Marvel gave Harris permission to purchase navy sailor hats and white duck trousers, a salute to the band's origins and its use of surplus military equipment.[62] Thus, for $13.50, Harris purchased three dozen sailor hats three days before the game.[63]

Newly uniformed, twenty-six of thirty men showed up, and the band was featured in a full-page *Providence Journal* pictorial.[64] On May 16, the now thirty-three-member band christened the new baseball stadium, Aldrich Field. It marched onto the field and played "The Star-Spangled Banner" and the Brown and Dartmouth "Alma Maters."[65] Such performances continued to garner widespread publicity and popularity for the band, creating momentum as it proceeded into its first full season as a group, 1925–26.

Earliest photo of the Brown Band, 1925. *Brown University Archives.*

To prepare for this season and ensure the band's survival, Harris took a conducting class at Columbia University during the summer.[66] The first football game of the season on September 26 against Rhode Island State was quite the sight, as the university athletic department had gifted the band a new bass drum, described as "the largest solid shell bass drum in New England."[67] The game took place in the newly constructed Brown Stadium. In the week following this game, wool musical letter sweaters were distributed to band members, courtesy of the athletic department. The white sailor hats remained, but the uniform top was changed to these sweaters.[68] Harris's commitment was clear, and this, combined with the bass drum and the new uniforms, signaled an important message to the Brown community; as the *Brown Daily Herald* pointed out, the new sweaters proved "that the band [was] here to stay, and to fill a long-needed vacancy in Brown activities."[69]

The most significant event that football season was the christening of the new stadium on October 24. With Brown coming off of a 48–0 win on the road against Bates, the excitement had built up even more for this day. Twenty-seven thousand fans were in attendance to witness the opening ceremonies, which featured both the Brown and Yale bands.[70] The Brown Band kicked off the ceremonies by performing "Hail to the Chief" as Governor Aram J. Pothier entered and "For He's a Jolly Good Fellow" for Mayor Joseph H. Gainer. Comically, during the first selection, half of the band repeated from the beginning of the song, while the other half repeated from the chorus. A Brown professor's wife in the stands was overheard saying, "My, isn't the Brown Band great; it is actually harmonizing 'Hail to the Chief.'"[71] The bands combined to begin their performance, led by Yale bandleader Roland B. Guild, with Irving Harris in tow. At the east goalpost, the bands turned and led the crowd in "The Star-Spangled Banner"; in turn, each crowd followed by singing their respective school's "Alma Mater" while the band looked on.[72] Impressed, the *Providence Journal* writers noted their thoughts on Brown's band: "In an almost unbelievably short time it has grown from a mere handful, unbalanced and poorly equipped, to a balanced and thoroughly trained band worthy of its Alma Mater."[73] Unfortunately, the great dedicatory ceremony did not help Brown overcome the excellent play of Yale, who won 20–7.

Following the football season, the band performed various concerts at venues like Butler Hospital and the Providence Biltmore and even performed over the radio on station WJAR.[74] In March 1926, the band announced that engineering professor Samuel J. Berard was appointed

Left: The band's first bass drummer, John Henry See, 1926. *Brown University Archives.*

Right: One of the band's first snare drums, played by J. Marshall McGregor '27. The drum was purchased from McGregor's daughter by the author in 2023. *Author's private collection.*

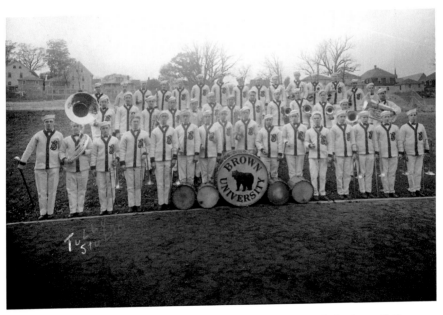

The Brown Band before the stadium dedication, October 1925. *Author's private collection.*

Samuel J. Berard, the band's first faculty advisor. *Brown University Archives.*

its faculty advisor. Originally temporary, Berard would remain in the position until his retirement from the university in 1945.[75] Less than three weeks into his term, Berard already had some mischief to deal with. During the band's March 26 performance at the Biltmore, a porcelain sign for the British Empire Club was destroyed, and so the band was blamed. While both Harris and Strauss proclaimed the band's innocence in letters to President Faunce, they reluctantly agreed to pay the replacement cost of fifteen dollars. Harris humorously wrote, "It was on canvas with a cheap frame and the printing was quite good. However, if the Club paid fifteen dollars for it they must have bought a half interest in the concern. I've done quite a few signs myself and would value it at a few dollars."[76]

May 1926 saw the beginning of a Brown Band tradition: its annual banquet, now known by the portmanteau "bandquet." It was first held on May 18, 1926, at the Providence Biltmore. The band celebrates its departing seniors and recognizes the past season at each dinner.[77] Early bandquets were more formal than present ones, and guests in attendance at the first one included university officials like Athletic Director Fred W. Marvel and Dr. Samuel T. Arnold, Director of Student Activities. Gold charms were awarded to the bandsmen for their service.[78] The charms caused quite a stir in the Brown community, for "the presentation of such a large number of keys [was] unparalleled by other non-athletic organizations."[79] Currently, the bandquet is held in November, prior to the last home football game, and marks the term end of the outgoing band officers. The outgoing president recites a poem about the board's experiences of the past year, and band members perform comedic skits. At this dinner, the band awards three honors to deserving students: the Irving Harris Award (most outstanding band member), the Paul Maddock Award (nonofficer who has contributed most to the spirit of the band) and the Walter Axelrod Award (most outstanding first-year band member). See page 45 for Harris, 73 for Maddock and 82 for Axelrod.

The band played on through the 1920s, continuing to impress listeners. Most notable, however, are a set of recordings made by the Brown Band, who

BROWN UNIVERSITY BAND

TENTH ANNIVERSARY

BANQUET and DANCE
PROVIDENCE BILTMORE
FEBRUARY 16, 1935, at 6:30 o'clock   COUPLE FOUR DOLLARS

Above: A ticket for the 1935 tenth anniversary banquet at the Biltmore. *Brown University Archives.*

Left: Brown Band charm, 1938. *Courtesy of Raymond Butti, Brown University Archives.*

became the first musical group from Brown to be professionally recorded. On a trip to the University of Pennsylvania in October 1927, the band produced a phonographic 78 rpm record at Victor Studios in Camden, New Jersey.[80] The band left Providence by boat Wednesday evening and landed in New York on Thursday morning for concerts at the Horace Mann School and the Waldorf-Astoria Hotel. On Friday, the men traveled to Camden. Recording the band plus vocal accompaniment took three takes; the result was Victor Record #21017. Side A of the record features "Brunonia (As We Go Marching)," "For Bruno and for Brown" and "Ever True to Brown,"

The band in formation, 1920s. *Brown University Archives.*

while side B has "Brown Cheering Song," "Ki-Yi-Yi" and "Brown Victory March." All selections were arranged by Irving Harris.[81] Very difficult to find today, the record sold many copies among the Brown community and was even reissued in the early 1940s.[82] Digital versions of the songs were re-released on the Brown Band's seventy-fifth-anniversary CD in 2000. The band over its history has pressed five records and two CDs, published in 1927, 1948, 1974, 1979, 1987, 1993 and 2000.

After an incredible run as bandleader that saw membership rise to sixty and featured numerous accolades and successes, Irving Harris retired from his post at rehearsal on January 17, 1928, passing the baton to Leonard E. Werner '29. Strauss continued to serve as manager until the end of the semester before being succeeded by Leonard L. Oster '30. The *Liber Brunensis* of 1928 aptly notes of Harris, "One could sum up Irv's career in two short sentences. Before he entered college, Brown did not have a University Band. Now such an organization not only exists, but is one of the best-trained in the East."[83] This praise is certainly warranted, but there are others who are

An original pressing of the band's Victor record, from the estate of Irving Harris. *Author's private collection, gift of Richard Levy.*

Have You Heard the New Record

of

BROWN UNIVERSITY SONGS

as played for

THE VICTOR TALKING MACHINE CO.

by the

BROWN UNIVERSITY BAND

(55 PIECES WITH VOCAL CHORUS)

ORDER THIS STIRRING RECORD BY NUMBER
FROM YOUR LOCAL VICTOR DEALER

VICTOR RECORD No. 21017 - - - PRICE 75 CENTS

An advertisement for the band's Victor record, 1927. *Brown University Archives.*

The Brown Band before the UNH game, November 19, 1927. *Brown University Archives.*

Irving Harris conducts the band, circa 1926. *Brown University Archives.*

Members of the Brown Band, circa 1930. *Brown University Archives.*

responsible for the band's early success. Harris himself attributed the band's success to Strauss, as evidenced by an article from the *Providence Journal*: "The reason for it all, according to Irving Harris '28, of New York, the leader, lies in the personality and consistent work of Manager Joseph L. Strauss, Jr., '28, of Illinois. Mr. Strauss holds that all the credit should go to Mr. Harris, who leads the harmony makers."[84]

Chapter 3

ROWING WITH THE TIDE

FROM MARCHING TO SCRAMBLING

*T*he 1930s brought many challenges for the Brown University community and the world. The Brown family mourned at the beginning of the decade when retired longtime president William Herbert Perry Faunce died of heart failure at his Providence home on January 31, 1930.[85] Faunce had been a supporter of the band since its inception, having written many encouraging letters to Irving Harris the previous decade.[86] Despite the economic challenges of the next decade, the Brown Band continued to show its support for the student body at university athletic events. While band membership remained steady, the 1932 *Liber Brunensis* notes that "it was impossible to stage the annual concert and dance in Providence because of general economic conditions."[87] Nonetheless, the band persevered, keeping the community entertained.

June 1930 marked the inauguration of the Harris Band Trophy, an award still given annually to the band member who "has done most to promote the interests of the band."[88] The first recipient was trumpeter John O. Prouty '31 of North Scituate, Massachusetts. Prouty's name was engraved on a silver trophy cup, gifted to the band by Irving Harris in honor of his father, Abraham, whom Irv noted was "an ardent supporter and friend of the band."[89] Today, the award is known as the Irving Harris Award in honor of the band's founder. While the cup ran out of space for names in 1945, the award continues today in the form of a large plaque on display in the band's home, Fulton Rehearsal Hall.

Above: Brown Band, 1933–34. *Brown University Band.*

Left: Harris Trophy. *Courtesy of Raymond Butti, Brown University Archives.*

Opposite: Special guest drum majorette Betty Brown, 1940. *Brown University Archives.*

In February 1935, the band celebrated its tenth anniversary at its annual banquet at the Biltmore. Officials present for this momentous occasion were Brown Vice President James P. Adams, Dean Samuel T. Arnold, Athletic Director Frederick W. Marvel and Advisor Berard and Coach Thomas B. Gall. Additionally, Irving Harris delivered a speech relating the founding and early history of the band to its current members. Robert B. McLeod and Joseph B. Grossman were jointly presented with the Harris Trophy.[90] In just its tenth year, the band had already amassed a rich history, which would continue to grow in the coming decades.

During the Second World War, the band supported both Brown and the strong military presence on campus. A number of patriotic concerts were

given by the band and glee club through the school year and the summer.[91] The band even traveled to entertain troops.[92] Additionally, patriotic guests like Betty Ann Brown of the Ice-Capades were brought in as special "honorary drum majors" and donned outfits of red, white and blue.[93] Many Brown men left to serve, which affected the band's membership. By 1944, the band consisted of mostly navy personnel: "fifty Navy to three civilian members," as the band had merged with the Naval Drum and Bugle Corps stationed on campus.[94] The band was also unable to

CONCERT
By The
BROWN UNIVERSITY BAND
Assisted By
The B.U. QUARTET
FAUNCE HOUSE TERRACE
Thursday, June 1, 1944
at 1930*
Everybody Invited
In case of rain postponed
to June 2nd
* This means 7:30 p.m.

A poster advertising a band concert, June 1, 1944. *Brown University Archives.*

go to away football games in the 1943–44 season due to the rationing of gasoline.[95] Some Brown Band alumni lost their lives in the service, such as Everett Seixas '32, a former band manager, who was killed in action in Luxembourg on December 27, 1944, and is interred at the American Cemetery there.[96]

The band owed much of its success in the 1930s to its new coach Thomas B. Gall, known as "Major." Gall led the 243rd Coast Artillery Band in the Rhode Island National Guard, hence his nickname, coined by students. Owing to his military experience, Gall transformed the band and made its musicality and marching more precise. Sadly, Gall passed away on September 9, 1938, leaving the Brown Band without its venerable coach going into its next football season. But his decade of work left a strong impact on the group and "rais[ed] the undergraduates to a high standard of excellence."[97]

Gall's successor as coach was Jovite Labonte. Labonte was another military man, who directed the 118th Engineers Band of the Rhode Island National Guard. He also had studied music under the band's first coach, Roswell Fairman, and played in the Rhode Island Brass Band under the tutelage of Gall.[98] Labonte played a number of instruments, including French horn, bassoon and trumpet, which made him the perfect candidate to assist more inexperienced members of the band. However, Labonte's tenure was short-lived; he was promptly called into military service as World War II began.

To replace Labonte, the band called upon well-known Rhode Island bandleader Edward A. Denish, who would coach them through the war years. Denish had composed a number of pieces, mostly trumpet solos, and his band frequently performed at venues such as Cranston's Roger Williams Park. He also composed a new school song, "The Brown and White," though this song lost popularity in subsequent years.[99]

In 1945, Franklin O. Rose became faculty advisor, succeeding Professor Berard. Like his predecessor, Rose was an engineering professor. At the time, the band was part of the athletic department, with the athletic director having a large say in band affairs, though the band did perform concerts under the guise of the music department.[100] Rose sought to elevate the band's status as a student organization and establish it as part of the music department, a feat he would accomplish in January 1947.[101] Having accomplished his goal, Rose left his post at the end of the 1946–47 school year. Rose's son Franklin Jr. would enroll at Brown the next year and serve as the band's manager.

If the band were to permanently be part of the music department, its faculty advisor needed to be a music professor. Thus, the department eliminated Edward Denish's role as coach and hired Professor Martin J. Fischer in the fall of 1947.

Born in Sioux City, Iowa, on February 1, 1916, Fischer attended the Juilliard School and served in the U.S. Navy during World War II. He joined the Brown faculty as director of both the band and the orchestra and a full-time professor. Students recall him as a very friendly, down-to-earth professor who enjoyed working on Brown Band halftime show scripts with the band president in the Ivy Room or Sharpe Refectory. He had a remarkable career at Brown; though he stopped advising the band in 1967, he remained teaching until 1981. Fischer was especially responsible for transforming the Brown University Orchestra from a small, informal group to the excellent musical organization it is today.

Fischer's arrival signaled a new era. The musicians were equipped with new brown and white uniforms, and gone were the days of student conductors; it was "Marty" himself who conducted the band in their field shows.[102] The reorganized executive board now consisted of president, vice president, secretary and treasurer, and student drum majors still led the band in parades.[103] The band drastically improved musically and formed complicated formations that led to numerous accolades from the *Brown Daily Herald*.[104]

One of Fischer's first tasks as advisor was to help record an album of Brown University songs. In honor of the music department, Professor Arlan Coolidge sought to feature the university's band, glee club and chorus. He contracted with WOR records and asked Fischer to have the band perform three songs of his choosing.[105] Fischer turned to a notable composer of the time who had achieved recent success with his song "Syncopated Clock": Leroy Anderson. Anderson was working on future hit "Sleigh Ride" at the time. In 1946, Anderson arranged an orchestral medley of Brown University songs titled "Brunoniana" for Brown Night at the Boston Pops. Anderson initially agreed to arrange "Ever True" and "Brown Cheering

Left: Professor Martin J. Fischer. *Brown University Archives.*

Below: Brown Band marching, circa 1947–48. *Brown University Archives.*

Opposite: The band salutes Rhode Island, circa 1948. *Brown University Archives.*

Song" but unfortunately was forced to back out due to time constraints, as his publishers were pressuring him to finalize "Sleigh Ride" and arrangements of "Fiddle-Faddle."[106] New Jersey band director C. Paul Herfurth, author of the popular *A Tune a Day* books, was instead commissioned in April to arrange the songs, and recording took place on May 27, 1948. The band played the two aforementioned tracks and A.G. Chaffee's "Bruno."[107] The recordings were released in a set of three 78 rpm discs housed in a book that was simply titled *Brown University.*

Later that year, the band added a key part of its modern repertoire. As mentioned in the introduction, Fred A. Otis (class of 1903), who was avidly involved in music during his time as a student, composed the new school song "Brown Forevermore," which won an alumni songwriting contest. After a short rehearsal with the newly acquired parts, the band performed Otis's new song at the 1948 homecoming game against Western Reserve.[108] "Brown Forevermore" has since become a band staple as "Number 3" (or Brown Threevermore).

Early in 1949, the band began to regularly perform at basketball and hockey games, events they had only occasionally performed at previously.[109] Additionally, the band enacted a new constitution in 1949 to remove tryouts

Brown Band, 1947. *Brown University Archives.*

and make the group more inclusive for prospective members.[110] These changes, though seemingly minor, signaled that the band had become an established presence in the Brown athletic community and that its continued growth required more membership.

The style of the band was also changing. Formerly a band focused on military-style precision, the Brown Band, like many of the Ivy League bands of the time, adopted a new style—the scramble band. The scramble band style's origins are unknown, with multiple schools claiming to be the first to adopt it in the 1940s or '50s.[111] Parodying typical military-style marching bands, a scramble band enters the field from the end zone, yelling and randomly scurrying around the field before members come together in a designated form. Accompanying this is a parodical script read over the stadium's public address system. Modern scramble bands have a more relaxed atmosphere than traditional bands, with the emphasis more on the entertaining script than on musicality.

It is unclear when exactly Brown's band adopted the scramble style. There may have been shows that had scripts but weren't entirely scramble style, or both may have come at the same time. There is evidence that the Brown Band had been involved in "stunts" on the field before, with one 1947 article noting a show against Holy Cross involving a blazing tuba and the "Bruno Fire Department."[112]

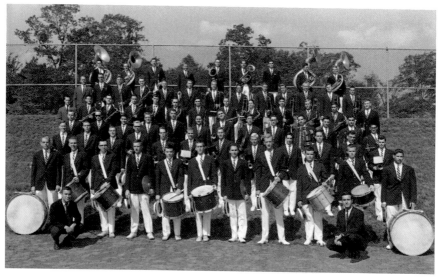

Top: The band salutes Brown Coach Rip Engle at the game against Western Reserve, November 6, 1948. *Brown University Archives.*

Bottom: The band changed its uniforms to a darker color in 1953. Here, the band poses for an official photograph, circa 1955. *Brown University Archives.*

Presumably making some sort of gambling reference, circa 1950. *Brown University Archives.*

The band scrambles, circa 1955–56. *Brown University Archives.*

The oldest surviving written halftime show script in the band's archives is from 1955. This points to the introduction of scripts slightly before then; in fact, the 1955 *Liber Brunensis* notes that in the previous year's football season, "the band created quite a commotion by parodying the entire Harvard administration," which suggests a script.[113] The band's membership declined between the mid-'40s and mid-'50s; though the 1950 *Liber Brunensis* notes a membership of seventy-five, the 1953 *Liber* notes the band was "small in size," while a later president recalled the band only being about thirty people or so. This decline likely caused the change in style; Fischer and his band board of officers wished to keep people who showed up to rehearsal coming to band events, so seemingly he'd be flexible with style, especially after the band had eliminated auditions the previous decade.[114]

Many of the early scripts were written and read aloud by Stuart Levine, AM '56, PhD '58, a French horn player. Levine studied at Harvard as an undergraduate, graduating in 1954. He alone may in fact be responsible for instituting the scramble band, if it is true that Harvard was the first to introduce the style. Levine was officially "Director of Halftime Shows."[115] The band president met weekly with Levine and Fischer to write the script. The week of the show, on Monday or Tuesday, the three would meet at the Sharpe Refectory dining hall in order to brainstorm the stunts they wished to perform "in order to prepare 'something' for Saturday" (as one recalled). Many alumni recall that Fischer gave the band mostly free rein when it came to shows, allowing them to have as much fun as they'd like—without crossing the line. The band adopted more of a relaxed atmosphere, and the university community, for the most part, supported it. Even President Barnaby C. Keeney once said to a group of band members walking down the street, "The team might be losing, but the band is really wonderful, and I really appreciate your efforts."[116]

A typical 1950s script resembles the following Princeton script. Visible is the band's punny style ("three-D classes") and its imagination through forming "only [the tiger's] tail."

1956 Princeton halftime show
Band marks time while announcer reads:
ANNOUNCER: This is the age of bigger and better. Automobiles have grown so long one can barely park them. Movies, while they may not be better than ever, are certainly bigger than ever. The Brown University Band has long advocated small-screen halftime shows, but progress is progress. The Band today proposes to stretch the football field out beyond

Marching up College Hill, 1950s. *Brown University Archives.*

its hundred yards. As a salute to Princeton, the Brown Band will form the largest tiger ever created. Stand back, friends, put on your three-D classes, and away we go.
Roll off into BBB [Brown cheering song] *and step off after intro. When band has stopped, announcer says:*
ANNOUNCER: And there you have it! A tiger so large the field cannot hold him. His body is directly under the Princeton stands, and his legs extend into the field outside the stadium. Unfortunately, only his tail is visible on the football field. (Now his shaking tail begins to wag)...and how we paws the Earth with his great claws! Too bad all you can see of this is his great tail wagging—but use your imaginations, friends—the [blank space] *hold no more.*
Roll-off into "B" then block for Alma Mater.

The earliest surviving script was read at Harvard on November 12, 1955. That day, the band performed a number of school songs, as well as Tom Lehrer's satirical "Fight Fiercely, Harvard."[117] What is omitted from the script is what the band decided on a whim to include at the end of the show. The band went past its allotted time, which angered the Harvard Band, which was waiting in the sidelines to run onto the field. Fed up with waiting, the Harvard bandleader made the decision to march the group onto the field, at which point the announcer read, "And now, ladies and gentlemen, the Brown Band proudly presents its second string," as the Brown Band scurried off the field, leaving the Brown fans laughing and the Harvard fans scowling.[118] These scripts often tried to push boundaries; in 1956, the band composed a script about the "sex life of the amoeba" but was forbidden to read it, not because of anything Brown had done, but because the Harvard band had caused a commotion at the previous weekend's show with a raunchy script.[119] Thus, it seems a number of the Ivy League bands at this time were actively straddling the censorship line.

It was at this time as well that the band resurrected its Irving Harris Award, the first recipient since 1947 being trombonist Ulysses "Jim" James '58, outgoing band president, on December 16, 1957.[120] James helped the band gain free tickets for their dates to attend football games, a larger budget for away games and improved facilities. He was a music major at Brown University and directed the Washington Metropolitan Philharmonic Association in Alexandria, Virginia, for thirty-nine years.[121]

The band forms a question mark against Harvard, 1958. *Brown University Band.*

The band often joined forces with the glee club for homecoming, prior to the election of the king and queen. They are pictured here in 1959. *Brown University Archives.*

Halftime shows continued to evolve. In October 1958, the band performed at the University of Rhode Island game. Tired of the standard halftime show, the Brown Band ended the show with a modernist and atonal version of "Ever True" composed by one member who later became a composer.[122] Such a unique stunt is emblematic of the Brown Band at the time. That year's Harvard show is a great example of the improvisatory, informal mood of the early scatter band. The band forgot its script at Brown, and so a replacement halftime show was written while en route to Harvard. "Ladies and gentlemen, as of 7:30 this morning, we had no show," the announcer's voice boomed as the band formed a question mark. Thanking the "inspiration of a beer bottle," the band saluted Harvard but noted that it was a small band and thus only able to form "HA." As a consequence, it played only a small part of "Ten Thousand Men of Harvard" and then marched off the field.[123] The following year at home, the band spelled out "HAR," as it now considered itself "of sufficient size to properly salute its neighbor on the north."[124]

While often noted for its political and social conservatism, the 1950s was a time when a new youth culture began to emerge. Signs of this are present in the shows described above, but this attitude would become increasingly evident in the following decade.

Chapter 4

PUSHING THE BOUNDARIES

THE SOCIAL CHANGES OF THE 1960s

*A*s the scramble band grew, it walked a fine line by seeking to insert double entendre and sexual innuendoes into each script. The band took pleasure in how many complaint letters it received each week. This attitude was a direct result of the transformative cultural revolution of the 1960s. With hippie culture flourishing, college campuses became places where a radical "No rules!" culture dominated.[125] Disdain for authority became more prevalent, leading on a national level to anti–Vietnam War protests and an increase in campus student protests. Curricula across the country became more liberal. Brown's "open curriculum" was born in 1968, allowing students the opportunity to take more electives and eliminating the core curriculum. Strict dormitory rules and curfews were abolished, and many schools began to explore the option of coeducation.[126] The increasing progressivism of the Brown student body evidenced itself in student activities, and thus the band's shows reflect this, intentionally or not.

As a result, the band's shows in the 1960s were occasionally controversial. In a 1960 show, the band formed an N and a K on the field, ostensibly referring to the upcoming presidential election of Nixon versus Kennedy, though many took the NK to also refer to Soviet leader Nikita Khrushchev, as the band played "Beer Barrel Polka." The band swapped the letters while performing to thirdly signify Ghanaian president Kwame Nkrumah, a nationalist authoritarian dictator. One 1963 halftime show attempted to advocate for fair housing for African Americans during the civil rights movement and referenced the racist actions of segregationist Alabama governor George Wallace. However, this show was inexplicably censored by Yale, with the athletic director calling it "not a proper subject," showing just how controversial some issues of the day could be.[127] One needs to look no further than the band's scripts to get a sense of the important political topics of the decade.

An example of the band straddling the censorship line was the 1966 University of Pennsylvania show, in honor of Pembroke College's seventy-fifth anniversary. The band formed the "stacks of the Rockefeller Library" and then asked, "When a Brown man refers to something as being stacked in the library, is he really thinking of his books?" and played "There Is Nothing Like a Dame."[128] Though not directly making an adult reference, the band's script and song choice together make clear to the aged listener its intent. However, references like these are not clear to children. Hence, these shows led to complaints from parents in the crowd but no disciplinary action from the administration.

Other shows were purely humorous; the 1965 Colgate show contained many toothpaste puns. The show began with the band on the sideline and the announcement, "In honor of Colgate the band has formed an invisible shield. In this formation the band has used 99% fewer members,"[129] a reference to Colgate toothpaste television advertisements. The script also noted the *Brown Daily Herald* was at the "crest" of its popularity.[130] Some found the band's new style unique; one op-ed author noted, "The Brown band concentrates its efforts toward some sophistication, rather than accepting the stereotype spectacle that is encountered at most inter-collegiate football games."[131] In 1968, the band notably had a halftime show in which all but a bass drummer remained on the sidelines. Miraculously, the one-piece symphonic band "formed" the Twin Towers, Times Square, Staten Island, Staten Island Ferry, New Jersey, the Holland Tunnel and the Washington Bridges for his confused audience.[132] The show was reprised in November 1970, much to the groans of the Columbia fans who thought it a sophomoric and dreadful performance.[133]

On a more serious note, 1964 was an important year for Brown and its band. Not only did the year mark the fortieth anniversary of the formation of the Brown Band by Irving Harris, but it also coincided with the bicentennial celebration of the university. In preparation for a special halftime show, the band president announced a reunion, inviting all band alumni back to perform. The band grew in size considerably that fall, adding 30 freshman members for a 93-person group. The new "band board" was very well organized with a much larger 10 members. Response

Drummers Steve Rost and Henri "Boom Boom" Bulterman, circa 1968. *Brown University Archives.*

to the notice was significant enough that 150 total marchers showed up for the October 31, 1964 homecoming and reunion show. The larger band, led one more time by Irving Harris, was able to spell out the word "Brown" stretching across the field at halftime. Harris returned with less hair but the same amount of spirit, sporting his original 1925 band sweater. John See '26, the band's first bass drummer, returned as well in full sailor uniform, as did band co-founder Joseph Strauss. Alumni enjoyed the reunion so much that 23 of them returned in 1965 for another reunion, an event that took place weeks after the band added to its résumé by performing at the New York World's Fair.[134]

In 1967, Martin Fischer stepped down as faculty advisor after twenty years to focus on the orchestra and teaching. He was succeeded by Frank Marinaccio, the first clarinetist of the Rhode Island Philharmonic and associate instructor in woodwinds at the university.[135] Like Fischer, Marinaccio took a laid-back approach with the band but focused on improving the organization musically as best he could.

His season would begin with a "bang." As there was no pushback from authority with the band's antic-filled halftime shows, there was no established "line" for the band to cross. This changed after the band's 1967 show at

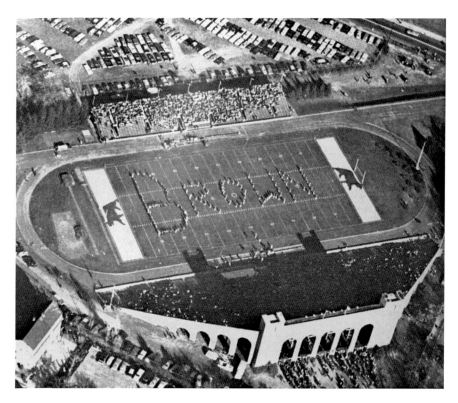

Above: The band and its alumni spelled out the word "Brown" during the show. *Brown University Archives.*

Right: Irving Harris, Homecoming 1964. *Brown University Archives.*

Right: Bass drummer John Henry See, 1964. *Brown University Archives.*

Below: The full band with alumni, October 1964. *Brown University Archives.*

Left to right: Executive Manager David Shoales '65, Strauss, Fischer, President Gordon Thomas '65 and Harris at the 1964 reunion. *Brown University Archives.*

Fischer (*right*) and Harris (*left*) conducting the band. *Brown University Archives.*

Numerous band alumni returned for the reunion, and some brought their families. Here, a little boy stands next to his father during the show, helping to form the *B* in Brown. *Brown University Archives.*

Fischer conducts the band at the 1965 World's Fair in Flushing. *Brown University Archives.*

Cornell. The crowd was already a little on edge going into the halftime show, as Brown had miraculously tied the score at 14 just before the end of the first half. Thus, the farming puns the show started out with in typical Brown Band fashion wouldn't be very popular:

> *Holy* **cow***! The Brown Band has gone* **hog wild** *making their first flight ever to the big* [time] *city of Ithaca.* **Hay,** *we really lofted our* **big bird** *in making it in one hour. . . . We thought Cornell was* **fodder** *away and almost flew* **pasture** *airport. But we* **tractor** *down and* **grazed** *in to a* **peas-ful** *landing. On the ground we* **herd** *some* **horse** *Cornell co-eds* **sheepishly** *singing.*[136]

However, in an incident recalled by many alumni as one of bad taste, the band then referenced Cornell's gorge suicides and played "I Want to Be Around to Pick Up the Pieces." Needless to say, this did not go over well with the Cornell fans, especially when combined with additional jabs at Cornell's hockey coach Ned Harkness. The band left the field to an incredible chorus of boos, while the band's script reader Paul Payton dodged projectiles thrown by angry fans into the press box. Cornell fans charged and rocked the bus as the band departed Ithaca, the band received a protest letter from the Cornell chaplain and the band board was called into the dean's office upon its return to Providence.[137]

In today's world, such a comment would lead to numerous complaints on a global level due to the advent of social media; however, in those days it was quite easy to get away with. The incident was so overlooked that the *Brown Daily Herald* ran no mention of the halftime show; rather, it included a letter to the editor from the band praising the football team![138] Since there were no established guidelines for the content of halftime shows, the band was not in any immediate trouble with Brown's administration. However, the dean of students enacted a policy requiring the band board to submit each script for review before each game. Doing so seemingly ensured that issues would not arise, though later bands found ways to circumvent this, as will be discussed.

Mentions of the Brown Band in the *Brown Daily Herald* are sparse during the late 1960s; this was mostly due to the increased focus on the social and political issues of the decade rather than campus happenings. Much like the Khrushchev/Nkrumah show of 1960 and the civil rights script that was banned from Yale in 1963, the band focused its scripts on a number of important, yet generationally divisive, issues. An October 5, 1968 show versus

Drum major Jay Ambrosini '67 smiles with a special guest drum majorette. *Brown University Archives.*

Penn saw the band draw influence from the 1968 Chicago riots. As a salute to "the great democracy that is America," the band formed *UAS* (instead of *USA*) on the field. Next, in the middle of the second song, a van drove onto the track, and two men dressed as police officers got out and "arrested" the student conductor, M. Robert Ment, as a jab at police reaction to student unrest.[139] (A copy of the script in the band archives humorously notes in a handwritten scrawl, "Ment didn't know what was going to happen.") Scripts also clearly reflected the liberalism that was beginning to sweep colleges. Following the election of LBJ in November 1964, the band drew ire from the Rhode Island Republican Party when it formed an *E* (a favorite formation for that year, in different contexts) for "the biggest elephant joke of the year—Nov. 3, 1964," a reference to the loss of Barry Goldwater.[140]

The new style of the band had its critics and supporters. One alumnus penned a scathing letter to university president Ray Heffner, specifically in response to the 1968 Penn show:

> *We have always felt that the Band…has never added to Brown's image in anybody's eyes.…This bunch of pseudo-sophisticated, semi-intellectuals should be prevented from representing and disgracing Brown again.…* [You should] *hire a new Band Director who will do away with the slapstick attitude that pervades this group of shuffling minstrels.*[141]

Another attendee wrote:

> *I think it is a unique type of band. I think it puts on a sophisticated show and that it would be a CRIME and a great loss should the Brown Band be forced to alter its mode of operation. The satire and spoof of the "big band" as done by the Brown Band can only be described as sensational.*[142]

Such differing opinions have defined the Brown Band in the decades since. However, perhaps the most significant positive change in Brown University history was the merger of all-male Brown University with its women's college, Pembroke. This occurred in 1971, but there were many gradual steps to the integration. By the time of the merger, classes were coeducational, and there were no longer any curfews for women; for all intents and purposes, Brown and Pembroke were unofficially united.

Traditionally, the band had been an all-male organization, as compared to the Brown Orchestra, which had been coed since 1940.[143] The band president in the 1966 season had attempted to admit women into the band, but the Pembroke administration refused.[144] As the merger grew closer, opinions on the matter changed, and in the spring of 1969, three first-year Pembrokers came before the band board and asked if they could join. These trailblazing women were Christine Curcio, Wendy Fredericks and Karen Kirby. The band board met and noted that there was no rule barring women in the band constitution, though there was no provision permitting them to join either. After a debate, the board held a vote. Of the five officers, three voted in favor, one voted against and one abstained.[145] The band officially became coed on March 16, 1969.[146] The biggest objection was that some band members felt they "could no longer be gross on the buses."[147] In their eyes, coeducation would significantly alter the existing culture of the band, forcing it to "clean up its act." In retrospect, they were incorrect; the band only became rowdier and raunchier, and many times it was women—in the years that followed—who were at the forefront of this.

Evidence for this continuity was present as the first coed football season was underway that fall. At the Yale show on October 11, "that all new razzamatazz damn co-ed band" saluted underdogs throughout history, including Christopher Columbus (forming a St. Christopher medal), American Indians (peace pipe), the New York Mets (bottle of champagne) and "the Yale Co-Ed, a group that we feel are truly underdogs," as Yale University had just allowed women to enroll. The band formed a woman on the field, and while playing "Another Opening, Another Show," moved the hem line of her skirt north to an extremely short length to "convey the idea of emancipation," once again pushing acceptable boundaries.[148] It quickly became abundantly clear that there was no need to worry about a possible change in the atmosphere of the group.

In anticipation of the November 15 game, the Brown Band was determined to outshine its Harvard counterpart. The Harvard Band is famous for its large bass drum on wheels with diameter of approximately eight feet. One student came up with an idea to build a wooden bass drum larger than Harvard's on the Thursday before the game. The band bought a junk Volkswagen chassis and built a wooden platform on top of it. Meanwhile, sousaphone player Kenneth Sloan '69 drove to a nearby fabric mill and bought its entire stock of cheap muslin. The recently joined three Pembroke students were recruited to sew together the muslin in order to form drumheads. On the eve of the Saturday game, several students pulled an all-nighter to execute the plan.

The result of the night's efforts was a roughly fifteen- to twenty-foot-high bass drum, proudly emblazoned with "Brown University Band." In typical band fashion, painting the words on the drumhead actually caused a bleed through to a third-floor room in Faunce Student Center, which remained there for years. When completed early in the morning, the drum was tied to a car's front bumper to maintain control when going downhill. However, the drum was *still* so large that two band members used long wooden poles

Before the band became coed, band members could bring their dates to games. Seen here is the band playing at a hockey game, circa 1969. *Brown University Archives.*

to push the low-hanging electrical wires out of the way as the band marched with its latest creation to the football stadium. The drum was hidden behind trees next to the visitor's side stands and was wheeled out to thunderous applause at the beginning of the halftime show, as the band played Fucik's "Entry of the Gladiators" and announced Knowles "leading, for the first time anywhere, the world's largest—baritone sax section."[149] Alumni credit the drum with sparking Brown to a 24–17 comeback victory that game, in a season where they went 2-7 overall.

Pride was a huge factor in generating favorable alumni opinion amid any controversies. Despite all of the changes in the band's personality, it did remain "ever true" to Brown. At the October 19, 1968 game at Dartmouth, the band braved a torrential downpour, despite the football team eventually losing 48–0. One notable Brown alumnus, Paul Lacoste Maddock '33, happened to be in attendance at that game. Inspired, Maddock endowed an award that continues to be presented to the member who is not an officer and has contributed the most to the spirit of the band. Additionally, Maddock donated a set of ponchos to the band to help keep them dry from the New England weather. The award was first presented in 1969 and was presented in 2018 to the author and his friend Zachary Goldstein.

The band added to its whimsical antics when it began to produce small pinback buttons in 1967, a beloved tradition that continues today. These buttons are distributed to fans at each football game, and band members proudly collect them. Buttons are a sign of seniority; those who have the most diverse collections of buttons have been in the band the longest. Each button pokes fun at the opposing school, either through stereotypes or sophomoric puns. The first button was JAM THE RAM, an anti-URI pin produced in 1967. The architect behind the idea was Kenneth Sloan, whose cousins ran a badge-making company. In the first year of manufacture, buttons were made for only some games. They became immensely popular, so the band produced buttons for each game the next season. This spontaneous idea morphed into a popular tradition that has continued for over fifty years. Fans love the buttons, with many longtime Providence residents possessing large personal collections. Other Ivy bands also collect the buttons and decorate their uniforms. To many fans, Brown football games would not be the same without band buttons.

With the addition of the buttons came a gradual trend toward more expressive uniforms. In the 1960s, the band wore navy blue blazers with boater hats, ties and white khakis. By the 1980s, the band wore brown wool sweaters—much more casual than the ones from the 1920s—and began to

Left: "World's Largest Bass Drum," 1971. *Brown University Archives.*

Below: The Brown Bear has some fun on the field as bandies look on, 1960s. *Brown University Archives.*

A collection of old band buttons belonging to Marvin Wasser '71. *Photo by the author.*

wear rugby shirts at some events. Today, the band's football season uniforms are brown blazers with a "Brown Band" patch on the left breast pocket with tan khakis, a style adopted in 1993. However, these blazers are adorned with dozens of the plastic buttons and often feature funny add-ons, such as the tiger tails sold by the Princeton University store, purchased by band members when the band travels there. They certainly are more personalized and reflect the change in social acceptability over time.

Depicted on the blazer's uniform patch is the band's mascot, Elrod T. Snidley. Elrod was first sketched as a self-portrait of band president C. Douglas Ballon '69 for band letterhead and nicknamed "Doogi," but

A flyer encouraging students to vote for Elrod Snidley, 1988. *Brown University Band.*

his name soon changed, supposedly first appearing as a band member's attendance sheet pseudonym. In 1988, Snidley, despite being just a mascot, ran as a write-in candidate for president of the Undergraduate Council of Students. A letter from fictional university registrar Josiah S. Carberry "confirmed" Snidley's enrollment, but though he defeated candidate Michael Dearing, securing 441 of 868 votes (50.8 percent), UCS ruled his candidacy invalid because he was not in fact a real person, let alone a registered undergraduate.[150] The band also enters intramural sports, trivia contests and similar events under the team name "The Elrod Snidleys." Between halftime shows, the buttons, and Snidley, the quirkiness of the band became quite apparent at the end of the decade. This pattern would only continue at the beginning of the next decade, when a new type of band performance was introduced.

Chapter 5

A "GREAT MUSICAL EXPERIMENT"

NATIONAL FAME FOR THE BAND

A marching band on skates?

The beginning of the new decade brought a new band tradition: the ice-skating band. Striving to do something new, the band officers asked the athletics department if the band could perform a shorter version of a halftime show on ice skates at hockey games.[151] In the past, the band had played at hockey games, even back in the 1930s, when it furnished music for students to skate to after the game.[152] Hockey coach Jim Fullerton was a big supporter of the band, so the idea was approved. The Brown Band remains today the self-proclaimed "world's only ice-skating band." Some marching bands perform on the ice in sneakers, but the Brown Band is the only band that actually ice skates while playing.[153]

The band first rehearsed its ice show on February 7, 1970, in Meehan Auditorium. Some found skating difficult, others not so. Footage from local news station WJAR shows some shakiness in band members, as well as a few members who, due to nerves, played small instruments like the tambourine. The end of the reel captures one band member completely wiping out, the first of hundreds, if not thousands, of times that has happened.[154] One week later was the first ice performance during a game against the University of Pennsylvania on February 14. As it was Valentine's Day, the band formed a heart on the ice during the show as it performed between periods.[155] The show was a great success, and the skating band continued to wow spectators throughout the decade, earning numerous accolades. The *Boston Globe* noted after one performance: "Although Harvard escaped Brown's Meehan

Left: Close-up of the drummers during a Valentine's Day–themed ice show, 1970s. *Brown University Archives.*

Below: The band's first ice show, 1970. *Brown University Archives.*

The band in motion on ice, February 6, 1988. *Brown University Archives.*

Auditorium with the victory, the Brown band (assuredly the nation's best skating college hockey band) put on a better skating show than Harvard."[156]

Today, a typical ice show begins with the performance of two or three pop songs. In between songs, the band skates into a new formation. Next, the band skates to the left side of the rink and forms two parallel lines. While performing the school song "In the Fray," these two lines skate forward and then cross paths in a "counterskate." The two crossing lines ultimately form a *B* in the center of the rink, and the show ends with the band skating around the rink counterclockwise while playing "Ever True to Brown." The shows were originally between periods but now take place after the games, due to a timing change by the NCAA.

In the fall of 1970, John Christie was hired as the new faculty advisor of the band, a position he served in until his departure in 1984. Many alumni fondly recall Christie, who allocated power to the band board but conducted shows himself, with a strong emphasis on musicality. As a student, Christie was a member of the University of Michigan Marching Band, which has a significantly different style than the Brown Band.[157]

John Christie also led the newly revitalized Brown University Wind Ensemble. The original Brown University Wind Ensemble had formed in 1959 from a combination of Brown and Pembroke musicians.[158] Under Martin Fischer's direction, it performed a number of symphonic band concerts after football season. A smaller Junior Band was run by Farrell

The band demonstrates its counterskate during its sci-fi-themed ice show, February 2016. *Brown University Band.*

John Christie and his wife enjoy the game. *Courtesy of Irv Lustig '83.*

Christie conducts the Brown Concert Band at Commencement 1983. *Courtesy of Rosie Perera '85.*

B. Fleming '62 and was composed of approximately fifteen players who were inexperienced but wished to improve. These groups ceased to exist by the middle of the 1960s. Edward Guiliano '72 was responsible for the group's reinstatement and served as its first president. The group's first performance was conducted by Czech-American composer Václav Nelhýbel on March 29, 1971, with a program of Nelhýbel's works. It continues to exist today as the Brown University Wind Symphony, directed by percussionist Kevin Plouffe.

Much in line with the skating band, antics did not cease in the new decade. The large bass drum that the band had built was also rolled out for the 1971 Harvard game, to thunderous applause. Unfortunately, following the game, an arsonist set fire to the drum, leaving the band without a prop for the 1973 Harvard game. That November, the band hatched a scheme that would go down in its history as its most notable stunt ever performed. The band president, Daniel Zemel '74, was its ringleader; assisting him were three other young men. The "Foxboro Four" (as they were later deemed) wanted to pull a special stunt because the football team had a winning record going into the Harvard game, and the winner of the contest would temporarily be in first place in the Ivy League standings, a rarity for Brown. The four men decided to steal the "world-famous" Harvard bass drum.

The Foxboro Four heard that the game was going to be broadcast as the New England game of the week on regional ABC television. At the time, Brown's student radio station, WBRU, was an ABC news outlet. Using material from the station, the four men forged ABC sports press passes. They piled into a pickup truck and drove to Cambridge, telling the Harvard band that they were ABC reporters who wanted to take photographs of the Harvard drum in order to show it on television during halftime of the football game.[159]

After successfully convincing the Harvard Band with their disguises, the men loaded the drum into the back of the pickup truck, claiming they were going to drive it to the field in order to take pictures. The Harvard Band librarian, later an Arizona congressman, insisted on coming along and having his picture taken with the drum. The men drove to the football stadium and then claimed that their scheme was all a prank and they were taking the drum back to *Yale*.[160] As one writer said: "Gleefully waving back at honking motorists, the drum abductors with their all-too-conspicuous, 72"-diameter Crimson Drum suddenly noticed that one of the vehicles was a state trooper's car with flashing beams."[161]

Caught by the state police on I-95 at the Massachusetts state line, the men were arrested and imprisoned in the Dedham County Jail before being bailed out later that night. That weekend's script made fun of the incident, and ABC TV commentators mentioned it on the broadcast.[162] After a month, the case was dismissed by the trial judge (who, as recollected by Zemel, was both a Brown graduate and a Harvard law graduate), and each member of the Foxboro Four agreed to pay twenty-five dollars in court costs, with no notation on their permanent records.[163] The prank became so prominent in Brown lore that it was even mentioned in Martha Mitchell's *Encyclopedia Brunoniana*, published twenty years later![164]

This decade also saw the band begin to record again. In May 1974, the band released an album in honor of its fiftieth anniversary. One thousand copies were pressed of a double-sided LP that consisted of twelve Brown songs, five pop songs and a medley of songs from other Ivy League schools.[165] Five years later, the band released another album titled *Ladies and Gentlemen, Friends and Alumni*, a reference to the words that typically begin each halftime show script. The repertoire featured on this album was very similar to the previous one, except it contained classical songs like "1812 Overture" and "Can-Can."

Beginning in 1975, the band also recognized the first-year band member who contributed the most to the organization. The Axelrod Award was first presented in 1975 and is named after Walter Axelrod '40, who was assistant leader of the band from 1939 to 1940 and, after graduating, operated a prominent music store for many years in downtown Providence at 251 Weybosset Street. Voting for the Axelrod Award usually takes a long time because each first-year band member must be nominated by peers before the election.

As discussed in the last chapter, censorship of Ivy League band shows, which began leaguewide around 1968, was now quite prominent. Much of this was due to pressure from alumni and angry letters from audience members.[166] Despite the fact that band shows were now censored and edited by Brown's athletic director, Ferdinand "Andy" Geiger, the scriptwriters still found ways to sneak double entendre and other suggestive themes into the scripts. In 1973, Geiger mistakenly approved one band show that was "a clinical analysis of human reproduction."[167] Protest letters were mailed to university president Donald F. Hornig and the band board. When Geiger resigned in 1975 to take a job at Penn, the band saluted him by forming his initials (F.A.G.) on the field and then saluting the new athletic director, Bob

The band's "toga show" against University of Rhode Island, September 30, 1978. *Brown University Archives.*

Ice show, December 11, 1981. *Brown University Archives.*

Seiple, by forming B.S.[168] In 1978, the band reused an old trick and built another large bass drum for the Harvard game, which was rolled out as the announcer introduced the "Anything you can do we can do bigger" band.[169]

These shows were never intended to offend anyone; they were merely meant to parody opposing schools in a lighthearted manner. They are representative of the 1970s college atmosphere; the older generation was insulted, while the younger generation thought it hilarious and good-natured. When asked about the shows, one professor wrote, "I find them occasionally tasteless, gauche, and infantile. But they're never offensive." Buddy Cianci, mayor of Providence and frequent supporter of the band, was quoted as saying, "I don't think they're offensive. They're refreshing, as a matter of fact."[170]

The 1980s marked a time when the band gained fame on a national level—for both positive and negative reasons. As the line between what was offensive and what was acceptable remained blurred, there were still moments of audience dissatisfaction, none more infamous than the band's September 26, 1981 halftime performance at West Point. Sporting buttons that read NUKE ARMY, the band's parodical style did not mesh well with the stern attitude of the United States Military Academy. When the announcer ordered the band to drop down and give him twenty, instrumentalists responded by pulling money out of their wallets for collection. Next the announcer remarked, "You know, West Point has come a long way. In 1980, it graduated its first woman. We can't wait until it graduates its first man."[171] From there, the band pretended to take orders, which included rubbing their stomachs and patting their heads while marking time. The show ended with, "Next week, come back with us to Providence to see the Brown University Army Band dishonorably discharge its privates."[172]

Both the performance and the report of the show that was published in *Sports Illustrated* on October 12 led to a slew of letters from alumni and attendees.[173] The university defended the band, though University Relations internally condemned the group's actions, calling it "sheer stupidity."[174] One attendee claimed, "The deplorable charade and disgusting script used by the Brown announcer should never have been presented,"[175] while another called it "the most tasteless half-time show I have ever seen."[176]

Others supported the band, with one notable defense coming from a West Point cadet: "If you cannot joke about yourselves, who can you joke about? One of the virtues of the band, as representatives of Brown University, is that it can lampoon the serious things in life, and let us all know there is a lighter side to everything."[177] As a result of its show, the Brown Band, like some other Ivy League bands that performed at West Point around that time, was permanently barred from the campus. The Brown Band's show is a far cry, however, from the Columbia band's performance at West Point a decade earlier, in which they formed "a burning Cambodian village" on the field, which is a far more insulting performance that took place *during* the Vietnam War and *deliberately* attacked the United States government and its military action.[178]

Ironically, the West Point show took place one day after a *Wall Street Journal* article appeared about school administrations strengthening censorship of troublesome Ivy League bands.[179] The article, "Ivy League Bands Keep on Marching to X-Rated Tunes," listed a number of recent infractions. The Yale Band ended a televised 1977 halftime show with band members pulling down their pants, revealing diapers. The Harvard Band in one instance parodied the Iran Hostage Crisis with "Shah Wars: The Persian Empire Strikes Back" and made multiple puns on the word "Shiite." Despite the strict censorship policies in place at many schools, controversial performances still slipped through the cracks. Many Ivy League administrators, conscious of the feelings of alumni, threatened their respective bands with sanctions or a complete ban if they did not clean up their acts.

While the Brown Band was not in any immediate danger of being defunded, the negative publicity directed toward the Ivy League bands demanded action. What emerged from this was the Ivy League Bands Conference (IBC), established by the University of Pennsylvania Band in April 1982.[180] This annual conference gives student representatives from each of the bands a chance to discuss with one another any problems from the past year, as well as plans for the future. Among the positive consequences of IBC have been the adoption of hosting policies by most of the Ivy bands, allowing visiting groups to stay overnight on campus, thus eliminating hotel costs, as well as a general consensus as to what is considered appropriate content for a halftime script. The inaugural conference led to the following policy statement, unanimously adopted:

> *We, the leaders of the Ivy League Marching Bands, recognize the importance of our organizations for school spirit, and alumni and public relations. We feel that both cooperation with and support from our school administrations are vital to the production of quality entertainment at intercollegiate sporting events. Recognizing and encouraging the diversity of our organizations, we believe we have a valid place within the framework of Ivy League Athletics. We acknowledge past concerns, and accept responsibility for the role we play in the educational processes at our respective institutions. A spirit of cooperation among our bands has been established and will continue.*[181]

Such a publicly announced desire to improve was welcomed and actually helped the band fundraise to secure new uniforms for the 1982 football season: Brown sweaters with a bear patch on the breast.

Other shows of the time were a hit with fans. The band traveled to Holy Cross College, poking fun at the name "Holy Cross" with a Batman-themed show. Two band members dressed up as Batman and Robin, attempting to deduce the secret identity of the Brown Band. The band formed the word *SIN*, which changed to *COS*, with Batman noting that the band's derivative was alcohol. As the band formed two halves of a potentially offensive formation on opposite sides of the field and began to push them toward each other, Batman and Robin saved the day by straightening the lines, thereby preventing "thousands of innocent women and children" from being offended and poking fun at the recent demand for censorship of Ivy bands.[182]

Lawrence Rosenbaum '85 dressed up as Batman for the Holy Cross show, 1981. *Courtesy of Lawrence Rosenbaum '85.*

The Brown Band marches to the stadium in the 1980s. *Brown University Archives.*

In the summer of 1984, John Christie unexpectedly resigned, and later that year, Matthew McGarrell was appointed director of bands at Brown, a position he held until 2019. McGarrell, a trombone player, had previously directed the Northeastern University and University of New Hampshire bands, which were much more serious organizations than the Brown Band, but he quickly adjusted to the student-run, irreverent group. Like his predecessor, Matt conducted the band's field shows. He commandeered the wind and jazz ensembles and helped transform those groups into the spectacular organizations they are today.[183] He also arranged a number of Brown songs for the band, as Christie had taken his arrangements with him when he departed.

Matthew McGarrell conducts, 1989. *Brown University Archives.*

One of McGarrell's first performances was the band's sixtieth-anniversary show on October 13, 1984, against Penn. Twenty-seven band alumni returned to scramble on the field. Notably, one alumnus was trumpeter John O. Prouty '31, the first winner of the Harris Trophy, who returned at the age of seventy-five, as fit and spry as ever. The band formed the Brown crest (or something resembling it) on the field and played the "Alma Mater."[184] The "Dueling Bandshow" (a play on "Dueling Banjos") at home against Dartmouth on November 10 was also a great success. McGarrell and his student conductor David Morse were dressed exactly alike, with similar hairstyles and beards, and carried cap guns to duel each other. All this happened while two announcers in the PA booth took turns reading, creating pure chaos. One student recalled, "We may have been the first band ever to play two unrelated songs at the same time on the field."

The band gained national fame on October 17, 1985. In a segment on NBC's *TODAY* called "Battle of the Bands," the Brown scramble band was featured alongside the University of Michigan marching band as part of a two-hour-long episode in which various aspects of the Brown and Michigan campuses were compared.[185] Michigan was featured first, with its players all neatly dressed in matching uniforms, perfectly in sync and musically excellent. One could only imagine the shock on viewers' faces when Jane Pauley introduced "The Great Musical Experiment—I mean,

Student conductor David Morse and Matthew McGarrell at the "Dueling Bandshow," November 10, 1984. *Courtesy of Rosie Perera '85.*

Experience, the Brown Band." The camera cut quickly to announcer Rick Perera '87 wearing a bear hat reading in front of a scrambling band on Brown's main green:

> *Good Morning America! It's the Brown University "We'll Teach You to Put us on Live Television" Band! We asked for Sixty Minutes on Sunday night, but only got one and a half on Thursday morning. Not being sure if we could form a Peacock on the air, we decided to form only half. We now enter a green pea formation to salute the Ivy League by playing "The Magnificant Seven" plus Cornell.*

Following the commercial break, Pauley noted that the switchboard in New York was "lighting up" with calls—an "unprecedented" event—and the Brown Band received an encore and played "Ever True."

Under McGarrell, the band recorded its next album, *Roadtrip*, in October 1987 over the course of a few rehearsals. As discussed in the *Brown Daily Herald*, "One of the biggest problems was that the band had to be absolutely quiet for 10 seconds before each song was recorded. 'We've never been quiet

YOU'VE SEEN US ON TV, NOW

JOIN THE BROWN BAND

- TRAVEL ON LUXURY MOTOR COACHES TO EXCITING & EXOTIC PLACES, SUCH AS HANOVER, N. H. & PHILADELPHIA, PA
- ENTERTAIN THE MASSES WITH MUSIC & HUMOR
- MEET FRIENDLY AND INTERESTING PEOPLE
- HAVE LOTS OF FUN!

-ANYONE WHO PLAYS AN INSTRUMENT IS QUALIFIED
-MARCHING EXPERIENCE IS NOT REQUIRED
-SIGN UP FOR AN INFORMAL AUDITION AT REGISTRATION
OR ACTIVITIES NIGHT, OR CALL MATT McGARRELL AT
863-3234 OR DARLENE NETCOH AT 861-7232 OR
AT FULTON REHEARSAL HALL AT 863-2110

Recruitment poster for the Brown Band, 1987. *Brown University Band.*

for 10 seconds before....I hope we can do it,' McGarrell joked."[186] The band's *Ladies and Gentlemen* album had become so popular that they had run out of copies![187] Like its predecessors, the album contains a number of pop songs and Brown songs. *Roadtrip* would be heavily marketed by the band in 1988 in honor of its sixty-fifth year, a year in which the band also got new uniforms, replacing their sweaters with rugby shirts.[188] Those rugby shirts have survived to the present day as the band's hockey uniform, matched with blue jeans. Together with all of this was the release and marketing of a ten-minute documentary video tape showing the band, originally created by Ben Hall '88 in 1986 for airing on BTV, the student-run television station.[189]

Band antics, of course, continued at the end of the decade, with band president Scott Perrin mostly responsible. As previously mentioned, band mascot Elrod T. Snidley was a popular candidate during the UCS election, securing a majority of the votes. During the 1988 football game at Princeton, the band dumped several gallons of bubble bath into the famous Princeton fountain, not expecting it would take several hours for the bubbles to form.[190] Later that month, Perrin and the band organized the "First Ever Great Brunonian Halloween Pumpkin Drop," dropping a

John Christie leads the band during the Gross National Parade, 1983. *Courtesy of Rosie Perera '85.*

Lawrence Rosenbaum '85 dons the bear costume during a later Gross National Parade. *Courtesy of Rosie Perera '85.*

Mayor Buddy Cianci receives bunny ears from Lawrence Rosenbaum '85. *Courtesy of Lawrence Rosenbaum '85.*

Buddy Cianci happily observes the percussion section, 1979, as snare drummer Karen Mellor '82 intently watches the conductor. Cianci has inscribed the photo "To the Best Band in the Ivy League and World—Good Luck—from Buddy Cianci, Cowbell Player." *Courtesy of Karen Mellor '82.*

twenty-two-pound pumpkin from the top of Sayles Hall to celebrate Halloween night.[191] Perrin originally wanted to drop the pumpkin from the Sciences Library, but university officials asked for a change in venue due to safety considerations.[192] An additional event that the band participated in four times during the decade was the Gross National Parade. This parade was organized by Washington, D.C. radio station WMAL and aimed to be silly. The first parade was in 1983; the Brown Band, not realizing the relaxed atmosphere of the parade, arrived in D.C. in full uniforms, only to find that spoofy acts like the Toro Toro Toro Precision Lawnmower Drill Team and the Briefcase Brigade were sharing the stage. The next year, the band wore costumes to better fit the atmosphere.

One big fan of the band's antics was Providence mayor Vincent "Buddy" Cianci, a frequent attendee of Brown football games. Cianci has become known in popular culture due to his ties to organized crime and political corruption, as detailed in season one of the popular podcast *Crimetown*, a popular biography by Mike Stanton and various other sources. Despite the corruption and his eventual prison term, his two separate mayoral terms, totaling over twenty-one years, resulted in a successful and prosperous city—and a large amount of support from the populace. Alumni fondly

Bill Barnert '78 (*left*) chats with Cianci at a 1979 game. *Courtesy of Bill Barnert '78.*

Band members pose with cymbal players Cianci (*front row, far right*) and university president Ruth Simmons, circa 2002. *Courtesy of Lauren Kupersmith '04.*

An elderly Cianci joins the band on cowbell one more time, 2008. *Courtesy of Karen Mellor '82.*

recall seeing Cianci playing either cowbell or cymbals in the Brown Band's percussion section for more than thirty years, beginning in 1976.[193] "I don't do bad for an old guy," Cianci quipped in one interview.[194] For a time, when he arrived at games, the saxophone section would play the theme from *The Godfather* as a reference to his organized crime ties.

Chapter 6

CANADIAN FLAGS
AND WAKING UP CAMPUS

THE BAND AS KEEPERS OF TRADITION

*A*s the band moved through the next decades, membership dropped, forcing the band to change. Maestro McGarrell stopped conducting field shows, leaving that instead to the student conductors, who took greater overall control of the group. The tone of halftime shows shifted away from some of the raunchy jokes and innuendos, due to the change in the band's sense of humor and the sense of humor of society in general. There was greater all-around intolerance for jokes that were now considered "offensive" or "hateful"—lines that might have slid by censors in the 1960s and '70s but wouldn't anymore.[195] By the end of the 1990s, auditions (which had made a loose comeback in the '60s) were no longer required to join; just basic knowledge of how to play an instrument was required. Ultimately, in 2017, the band rolled out a music lessons program, thereby allowing anyone to join even if they possessed no musical experience. The band's repertoire changed as well, as student conductor Jack Sheinbaum arranged multiple pop songs for the group in the early '90s, beginning a trend that continues into the twenty-first century. These pop songs, including hits like Nirvana's "Smells Like Teen Spirit" and Bruce Springsteen's "Born to Run," were featured alongside Brown songs on the band's 1993 album *Dusky*, its first CD release, named after McGarrell's dog.

In 2020, members of the Brown Band alumni Facebook page were asked to recall memorable events that they would want mentioned in a book. In a thread of over one thousand comments from alumni, one thing was clear: the alumni from the last thirty years overwhelmingly recalled the traditions

Part of the change in the band was in its instrumentation; seen here is one young member playing his violin. *Brown University Archives.*

of the band rather than halftime shows or other performances. In fact, the traditions and personality of the band have been the subject of campus newspaper articles in recent years more than ever before.[196]

Traditions are a core part of the Brown Band. No matter the extent to which Brown and its band change, or society changes, the band's traditions continue to be preserved and honored. This occurs for two main reasons. One, the band members seek to honor their predecessors through perpetuation of memory. As one student wrote, in the Brown Band, "Tradition is what happened when you were a freshman."[197] Freshmen are so awestruck when they first encounter the band traditions that they seek to replicate their experiences for new students when they become upperclassmen. Each band member learns the traditions through observation of others, while stories honoring former band members are passed down between generations of students.

Second, traditions have become such an integral part of the band that they have achieved normalcy. It is a running joke in the band that if anything happens twice, it becomes a tradition. Band members also have an affinity for attempting to create traditions. They occasionally perform irreverent actions in the hope that the band will find them funny and others will replicate the

Top: *Dusky* release concert, 1993. *Courtesy of Becky Feldman Sheinbaum '94.*

Bottom: A poster advertising the release of *Dusky*, 1993. *Brown University Band.*

action at a later date. Replication eventually reaches normalcy, and a new tradition is born. One can examine the band buttons, such an integral part of the group's culture—an aspect even recognized by the *New York Times*— that no one can imagine the group without today.[198] Therefore, it is quite appropriate to focus on traditions for the last part of this history.

In speaking with band members, one tradition was a clear favorite. A visitor to a Connecticut rest stop on I-95 on the Saturday of an away Brown football game could experience quite a surprise. Entering, he may find a group of students forming a circle around a Canadian flag in the center of the building, belting out the Canadian National Anthem at the top of their lungs. When the song concludes, the performers sprint out of the building. Despite their "Brown Band" polo or rugby shirts, the participants will insist that they are *not* from the Brown University in Rhode Island but the "Brown University in Canada."

Some observers sing along, some boo, but most stand there utterly confused. This tradition spontaneously originated around the year 1995 and has likely persisted due to band members' fond memories of the original impromptu occurrence, and thus is imitated every time the band goes to a rest stop. At one point in the 2010s, one driver disciplined the band for not

Members of the Brown Band show off their button-filled blazers at a game against Yale, 2017. *Courtesy of Yale Precision Marching Band.*

Warren P. Leonard '30 was bandleader in the 1929–30 season but returned to play his piccolo and conduct the band for a number of commencements in the 1990s. Leonard is pictured here conducting in 1991. *Brown University Archives.*

having a Canadian flag present when singing the anthem, and thus it is now the job of the corresponding secretary to bring that flag on trips.

Likewise, an odd yet popular tradition takes place every year at commencement. As the band leads the commencement procession through the gates, the band members turn around and hop on one foot backward while crossing their fingers and their toes. As soon as each member is through, he or she immediately reverts to marching normally as if nothing out of the ordinary had just occurred. According to Brown tradition, one is only meant to pass through the Van Wickle Gates twice—once entering during their first-year convocation and the second time leaving as a Brown graduate upon their commencement. As the band participates each year in commencement, its undergraduate members do not wish to tamper with tradition by walking forward through the gates, so they walk backward to make sure they are not cursed. A number of alumni traditionally join the band during commencement, as the band loses its senior members who are graduating. It is custom for former conductors to lead the band in at least one song during commencement weekend.

Perhaps the most poignant band traditions are the ones that take place within the group, away from the public scene. The Brown Band sings a large arsenal of songs while traveling by bus to away games. Historically, these songs have been parodies or insults to other schools. The bus songs are taught through oral tradition; only the appointed band historians have copies of the lyrics. No band member is authorized to record anything that is sung on the bus.

One such bus song is a parody of the Columbia University fight song "Roar Lion Roar." The song was originally taught in an alternate form to

Commencement band trombones spanning multiple generations, May 1998. *Brown University Band.*

the Brown Band by the Princeton Band.[199] This parody opens with ten verses making fun of opposing schools and then recounts a number of unfortunate experiences of past band members. However, examining some former verses of bus songs can tell a bigger story about history and politics. For instance, one former verse that has since been dropped speaks of the Soviet Union:

> *Roar, comrades, roar*
> *And let it echo through the halls of Moscow*
> *Fight on for oppression evermore*
> *All the sons of Lenin roam the tundra of*
> *Siberia, Siberia*
> *If they want rights we'll screw them*
> *Roar, comrades, roar*
> *Let's go out and start a nuclear war.*

As the Cold War is over and the Soviet Union no longer exists, this verse ceased to exist with it. Likewise, a verse about the Middle East discussed the oil crisis; a verse about Mayor Buddy Cianci parodied his ties to organized crime; and a verse about Persians discussed the Iranian Revolution and Ayatollah Khomeini. These verses were comedic in their own time and were especially relevant to current events. Today, society is far removed from the oil crisis, the Cold War and the Iranian Revolution. These verses are no longer relevant and thus were abandoned in favor of more recent events.

To this day, the great heist of the Foxboro Four, as recounted in the previous chapter, remains immortalized in oral tradition, to the tune of "Lizzie Borden" as performed by the Chad Mitchell Trio:

Last November up in Cambridge Harvard's bass drum disappeared;
What happened was the best we hoped and then the worst we feared.
But give credit to Brunonia and her great Foxboro Four—
When college pranks are mentioned, quote "New Haven nevermore!"

    But you can't steal a mascot up in Massachusetts.
    Not even if you're in the Ivy League (Ivy League);
    No, you can't steal a mascot up in Massachusetts,
    You'll only rest in jail for your fatigue.

For the game on television, Harvard was as psyched as we,
So we told 'em we could put their drum on ABC T.V.
The plan was perfect—Harvard swallowed sinker, line, and hook,
They stifled their suspicions and they loaded up our truck.

    But you can't steal a mascot up in Massachusetts,
    Though it's not made of silver nor of gold (nor of gold);
    Thou shalt not steal a mascot up in Massachusetts,
    Where Harvard's God, the Ten Commandments hold.

We got the drum to Soldier's Field and then we made our break,
And it seemed like here the coast was clear—we just made one mistake!
For we didn't know our turkey and left Coppersmith alone,
He may not be Clark Kent, but he went heading for a phone.

    But you can't steal a mascot up in Massachusetts.
    Without arousing Harvard bandies' fears [bandies' fears],
    No, you can't steal a mascot up in Massachusetts,
    You might end up with five to twenty years.

Well old Sam, he called the campus cops who called the state police,
They pulled our pickup over and we said we'd go in peace;
They threw us into Dedham jail then dragged us into court,
Well, who'd have thought that Harvard would be such a lousy sport?

But you can't steal a mascot up in Massachusetts.
Not even just to take it back to Brown (back to Brown);
No, you can't steal a mascot up in Massachusetts,
The state po-lice are sure to track you down.

With our fancy pants attorney there from up Pawtucket way,
We still wound up with court costs of a hundred bucks to pay.
But Harvard had to call the cops to even up the score;
They couldn't match the brilliance of the Brown Foxboro Four.

But you can't steal a mascot up in Massachusetts.
Not even if you've gone to case the joint (case the joint);
No, you can't steal a mascot up in Massachusetts,
Massachusetts is a far cry from West Point!

No, you can't steal a mascot up in Massachusetts,
Massachusetts is a far cry from West Point!

As it was such a prominent event in the band's history—one that was both locally and nationally recognized—it is important that it be retold to future generations.

No discussion of Brown Band traditions would be complete without mention of cheers. The band enjoys spelling out words, such as "S-C-O-A" (score, if you say it fast), and then spelling out words like "B-R-A" or "C-O-R-S-E-T," asking, "What's that do?" answered by the pro-defense "Hold 'em, hold 'em, hold 'em!" Other cheers originated from fans. One fan sitting behind the band once yelled at the top of her lungs, "GIVE THEM NOTHING!!" which one year later made its way onto the hockey season button. The more the band can make its presence known, the better.

On another occasion, a Brown soccer player yelled, "Shoes off if you hate Cornell!" while the band was on the bus to a Brown versus Cornell hockey playoff game with other students. This is a play on an anti–Manchester United chant, "Shoes off if you hate Man U." Hence, the band now chants this (while raising shoes in the air) at any game in which Brown plays Cornell and usually gets incredulous looks from confused crowd members. More than twenty years have passed from the initial occurrence, but the cheer still lives on as a tradition, as do a number of others. Naturally, as society changes, the cheers change. The band historians compiled a list of cheers around the year 2003. Of the twenty on that list (which is "by no means

The band members don their rugby shirts to play at the hockey game, 2019. *Brown University Band.*

complete"), only eight were still used at games in the 2018–19 season, and fewer since. Some cheers were removed because they were offensive, while others were not memorable and thus forgotten.

Though it has a multitude of supporters, the band still draws ire from some students. On the Saturday of Family Weekend each year, the band leads an 8:30 a.m. campus march, in which it plays in front of each dormitory, waking students up for the football game. In its pursuit of this activity, the band has had ice, window screens and other projectiles thrown at it from dormitory windows. One angry student created a Facebook group called "I f-cking hate the marching band" [censorship added] in response, which was infiltrated by the band within a week, with band members making fun of themselves in posts. In typical Brown Band fashion, band members now serve as the group's admins. The band also annually travels around campus in December, marching through dining halls and study spaces while performing holiday carols. While most of the students enjoy the holiday spirit, a few who are trying to study will verbally or visibly display their disgust.

The Brown Band in recent years has focused primarily on building up social activities. A biannual picnic, known nonsensically as "Flugenflagel" (a

On ice at the Providence tree lighting, December 5, 2015. *Brown University Band.*

Band picnic fun. *Brown University Archives.*

mutilation of "Haffenreffer," the original site of the picnic), introduces new members to the social atmosphere of the band at the beginning of the year and sends off the group's graduating seniors at its end. Using social media, the band's "social chairs" work to promote an inclusive environment that includes various weekend get-togethers. This has certainly helped to build a sense of camaraderie among the band members, one that continues to grow year after year.

The distinct culture of traditions attracts students to the band and encourages a strong sense of community. "One of the most appealing things to me when I joined the band was the fact that it was this organization with so many storied traditions," said Isabela Karibjanian '19. One scholar argues that by participating in traditions, undergraduates "feel a part of something larger than themselves."[200] College campuses are transitional spaces, and thus encountering traditions while transitioning into adulthood can have an enormous impact on one's life. Many band members remain lifelong friends, and most cannot imagine their college experiences without the Brown Band. Some band members even wed following graduation.

The band's traditions contribute to its attractive distinctiveness, both among Brown organizations and nationwide college bands. Trumpeter William Brakewood '22 aptly described the traditions as "ways for the band to be the band." There are many other historic organizations at Brown University that have their own rituals, but perhaps part of what is attractive about the band is that its customs are *not* static. Brakewood added, "The band has this element of, 'We've been around for a long time with these historic traditions,' but it's not a serious 'this is only how we do things.' It's just about having fun." This concept of it being a band tradition to change traditions, as societal and cultural shifts dictate, allows new members the ability to leave their own marks during their tenure, while participating in rituals that are central to their college experiences.

The focus on traditions by band members does not mean that there were no memorable shows during this time. The 2002 URI show was centered around the "Big Blue Bug," a fifty-eight-foot-long giant mascot for a namesake pest extermination company, visible on I-95. Ditching the normal band uniforms, the percussion section dressed up as the exterminators, while the rest of the band dressed up as the bug. The Brown Band's great relationship with the Princeton Band in recent years has led to a number of collaborations, such as an October 18, 2014 joint halftime show. Each band had its own PA announcer tell the story of "Brunoneo and Princetoniette," in the style of Shakespeare's *Romeo and Juliet.*[201] The show ended with the

Above: Lucas Sanchez '21 leads the band on its march to the stadium before the URI game, October 2019. *Brown University Band.*

Left: Band vice president Ingrid Mader '20 poses as she coaches the band during halftime show rehearsal, November 2019. *Brown University Band.*

Opposite: The percussion section dressed as exterminators at the 2002 University of Rhode Island game. *Courtesy of Lauren Kupersmith '04.*

birth of Johnny, the "love child" of the two bands, and the incredible stretch of a pun "**Johnny** will truly **B.** a **Goode** omen," introducing the Chuck Berry song to a series of groans from the crowd.

One milestone moment was in November 2017, when the band performed pregame and halftime shows at the Brown-Dartmouth football game at Boston's Fenway Park, part of Fenway's Gridiron Series. Scripts were not read due to lack of access to the Fenway PA system.[202] Frigid subzero temperatures made it difficult for sound to come out of instruments and also meant that most of the audience had left by halftime. Naturally, the band took advantage of playing at Fenway and performed "Sweet Caroline"; the Dartmouth band did the same. Band members took turns running to the bathrooms to warm themselves under the hand dryers during the second half. Nonetheless, a good time was had by all in the bundled-up band, despite Brown's painful 33–10 loss in a season that saw them go winless against other Ivy League teams.[203] The band's button for that game read "Big Green Monsters," a natural tie-in between the Dartmouth Big Green and the famous wall at Fenway Park.

In 2019, Matthew McGarrell announced that he was retiring at the end of the following school year. To ease the transition of power, he passed the baton over to Karen Mellor '82, the band's percussion coach, who became

Alexander Perl '18 and Francesca Lim '18 show off their Yankees pride at Fenway Park, November 10, 2017. *Brown University Band.*

the first woman to lead the Brown University Band as advisor. Mellor, pictured with Buddy Cianci on page 110 as a snare drum player, joined the band as percussion coach beginning in 1987 and has influenced hundreds of students since.

As it was for everyone, 2020 was a significant year for the Brown Band that led to challenges. Before the onset of the COVID-19 pandemic, the band did have quite the bright spot, as on February 14, 2020, it celebrated the fiftieth anniversary—to the day—of the Brown Band on ice. Alumni were invited back for the anniversary performance; Kenneth Sloan was the only member of the original skating band to return for the show but did so with great spirit and enthusiasm. The band during its performance invited the audience "to reflect…on how far we've come from five decades ago. You know, when ice was frozen, bands were terrestrial, and band alumni were men."[204]

Only a month later, the band's year would abruptly come to a close due to COVID-19. However, this did not stop the group from showcasing its Brown spirit. In honor of the class of 2020, the Brown Band and its

Karen Mellor and Matt McGarrell, 2019 commencement. *Courtesy of Karen Mellor '82.*

alumni virtually performed the Commencement March. Individual video recordings were made by alumni and submitted to the student conductors to be edited together. Instrumentation ranged from common instruments like flute and trumpet to improvised percussion instruments like washing machines. One might think that a pandemic could bring trouble for a very social group like the Brown Band—but no! In quite the opposite instance, the band continued to meet throughout the year through Zoom, organizing social events. During football season, the band met with members of the other Ivy League bands, in lieu of interacting with them at the scheduled football games, and it still produced buttons that were distributed later.

Before the 2023–24 football season, the band board made a significant announcement. After decades of being separate from, and occasionally at odds with, the Athletics Department, the Brown Band had once again officially become part of the department due to financial needs. Not only does this merger symbolize the band's importance to the campus community, but it also represents the desire of the band to have better communication with Athletics, to hopefully ensure a positive relationship in the years to

The band's percussion section, pictured here in 2018, annually plays its final cadence of football season by marching down the stadium's bleachers. *Courtesy of Karen Mellor '82.*

come. The change was negotiated by Mellor in conjunction with Brown's new athletic director, M. Grace Calhoun.

In 2024, the Brown University Band celebrates its 100th birthday and begins another century of hijinks. Much has changed in Providence since the university's founding in 1764, but few organizations have been as consistent with loyalty to Brown as its band. While the band creates its own songs, cheers and antics as part of its individual tradition, it also preserves the traditions of the university. The band's performance of the official school songs—even if the lyrics are modified or omitted over time—allows those songs to live on in campus memory and not fade into oblivion. Perhaps some of the current students at Brown don't know the lyrics to "Ever True," but they do recognize it as the school fight song when it's played, not realizing that it is over a century old itself. The Brown Band may no longer march onto the field like part of the military, nor dress for that occasion, but its core principles—instilled in it by Irving Harris all those years ago—continue to drive the group through continuity and change.

As the university continues to evolve, the Brown Band will remain a reminder of past tradition, an emblem of the current times and an example of the bright future that awaits the school and its future students. It is the author's hope that this account, while not a complete history of the band, will be one that serves to demonstrate how important the band is, and will continue to be, to Brown. When something is a part of campus culture for many years, it is sometimes taken for granted. Hopefully that will not be the case as the Brown Band continues to be "Ever True."

SONG LYRICS

"Ever True to Brown"
—Donald Jackson, 1909
We are ever true to Brown,
For we love our college dear,
And wherever we may go,
We are ready with a cheer,
And the people always say,
That you can't outshine Brown men,
With their Rah! Rah! Rah! and their Ki! Yi! Yi!
And their B-R-O-W-N.

— — —

"Brunonia's Big Brown Team" (Brown Cheering Song)
—Robert B. Jones, 1907 (words), and Howard S. Young, 1908 (music)
When Brunonia's Big Brown Team is in the game,
And the whole line is fighting to guard her name,
And the Bear growls like thunder as the backs crash by,
There's a killing on the Old Hill tonight.

Brunonia's banners are waving in triumph on the hill,
Brunonia's cohorts are cheering for the bear has made his kill (Rah! Rah!)
This day is Brown's, Brown's forever, let the vanquished count the cost,
So rise, rise and cheer, boys, till the last white line is crossed.

Come Freshmen and Sophomores, and Juniors too,
Seniors and Grads, well you know what to do;
Sing out this song, and give them your cheer,
While your team's down there plugging along
(this an alternate opening, quickly changed shortly after it was written, when
the song was rereleased as "Brunonia's Big Brown Team")

— — —

"BROWN FOREVERMORE"
—Fred A. Otis, 1903
Our boys are out there fighting,
As they never fought before.
They're crashing and they're smashing
To roll up a glorious score.
Let's give our ev'ry effort
And we'll help them go to town.
And we will all be happy
With a victory for Brown.

Let's give a cheer for dear old Brown, with its team of valiant men,
And raise our voices to the sky, so they will win again,
Let's back our team with all our might, to make a winning score,
Because it's fight, fight for Brown boys, and for Brown forevermore.

— — —

"FOR BRUNO AND FOR BROWN"
—John R. Bair, 1913 (words), and Donald Jackson, 1909 (music)
The name of Brown, boys, shall never fall,
'Midst the great or small, she is the best of all,
For her fair name, boys, we'll win the game,
And add another victor's crown.
So then we'll smash, crash against the line,
As in "Auld Lang Syne," crush them down!
Then cheer, boys, yes, cheer, cheer, cheer,
Just for Bruno and for Brown.

— — —

"ALMA MATER"
—James A. DeWolf, 1861
Alma Mater! we hail thee with loyal devotion,
And bring to thine altar our off'ring of praise;
Our hearts swell within us, with joyful emotion,
As the name of Old Brown in loud chorus we raise.
The happiest moments of youth's fleeting hours,
We've passed, 'neath the shade of these time-honored walls,
And sorrows as transient as April's brief showers
Have clouded our life in Brunonia's halls.

And when we depart from thy friendly protection,
And boldly launch out upon life's stormy main,
We'll oft look behind us, with grateful affection,
And live our bright college days over again.
When from youth we have journeyed to manhood's high station,
And hopeful young scions around us have grown,
We'll send them, with love and deep veneration,
As pilgrims devout, to the shrine of Old Brown.

And when life's golden autumn with winter is blending,
And brows, now so radiant, are furrowed by care;
When the blightings of age on our heads are descending.
With no early friends all our sorrows to share;—
Oh! then, as in memory backward we wander,
And roam the long vista of past years adown,
On the scenes of our student life often we'll ponder,
And smile, as we murmur the name of Old Brown.

— — —

"KI-YI-YI!"
—William A. Hart, 1903 (words), and Edward W. Corliss, 1895 (music)
We're loyal men of good old Brown, we're out to do or die,
And cheer our men to vict'ry with Our Ki-Yi-Yi.
Our team is made of heroes bold, who aren't afraid to try
And we are close behind them with our Ki-Yi-Yi.

Ki-Yi-Yi
Come and give a good and lusty!
Ki-Yi-Yi
For our team so tried and trusty,
Ki-Yi-Yi boys, come! Now!
Give them a good snappy Ki-Yi-Yi!

The green of Dartmouth, Williams purple, Blue of old Eli,
Fear the brown and snowy banner backed by Ki-Yi-Yi.
We don't care for Princeton Tigers, let the Crimson try.
They will fall before Brunonia's Ki-Yi-Yi.

(Repeat Chorus)[205]

— — —

"HERE'S TO GOOD OLD BROWN"
—Arr. by George Rosey
Here's to good old Brown, drink her down, drink her down.
Here's to good old Brown, drink her down, drink her down.
Here's to good old Brown, she's the jolliest place in town,
Drink her down, drink her down, drink her down, down, down.

Chorus:
Balm of Gilead, Gilead
Balm of Gilead, Gilead
Balm of Gilead, Way down on the Bingo farm;
We won't go there anymore, we won't go there anymore
We won't go there anymore, way down on the Bingo farm.

We left her with a sign, drink it down, drink it down.
And we'll love her till we die, drink it down, drink it down.
Here's to good old Brown, she's the jolliest place in town,
Drink it down, drink it down, drink it down, down, down.

Chorus.

Here's to profs and fun, drink it down, drink it down.
And to each true college son, drink it down, drink it down.

Here's to good old Brown, she's the jolliest place in town,
Drink it down, drink it down, drink it down, down, down.

Prexy,[206] here's to you, drink it down, drink it down.
For you're bound to put her through, drink it down, drink it down.
Here's to good old Brown, she's the jolliest place in town,
Drink it down, drink it down, drink it down, down, down.

— — —

"I'm a Brown Man Born"
—adapted from UNC
I'm a Brown man born, and a Brown man bred,
And when I die, I'll be a Brown man dead.
For it's rah, rah, Brunonia-onia, rah, rah, Brunonia-onia,
Rah, rah, Brunonia, Brown Brown Brown.

Oh, we licked Harvard and we licked Yale,
And there ain't no team that we can't whale!
For it's rah, rah, Brunonia-onia, rah, rah, Brunonia-onia,
Rah, rah, Brunonia, Brown Brown Brown.

Oh, we licked Dartmouth and we licked Penn,
And what is more, we can do it again!
For it's rah, rah, Brunonia-onia, rah, rah, Brunonia-onia,
Rah, rah, Brunonia, Brown Brown Brown.

Oh, we beat Harvard and we beat Yale,
We tied a knot in the tiger's tail!

Oh, we beat Dartmouth and we beat Penn,
But that was back in 1910!

Oh we lost to Rhody, we didn't come near.
We gave back the cup but first we drank the beer!

(Originally "Here's to Good Old Brown" was a separate song, but these two songs have merged over time.)

— — —

"(WHEN OUR MEN GET) IN THE FRAY"
—Alfred G. Chaffee, 1902

We fight, we fight with main and might, we fight like ancient warriors bold.

Again, again we cheer our men, as warriors did in days of old.

We fight, we fight for Brown and White, and mark the time with fife and drum.

Diddyum bum bum, Diddyum bum bum, Diddyum bum bum bum bum bum bum

Nicholas, Nicholas Brown.

When our men get in the fray,

We'll watch them play, and shout Hooray!

And we will help to win the day,

Another victory for Brown.

If perchance our men should meet

A bad defeat, there's no retreat,

For whether we're up or whether we're down,

We'll fill up the cup and drink to Brown,

And cheer, and cheer, and cheer,

Rah! Rah! for Brown! Rah! Rah! for Brown! Hey!

— — —

"BROWN BEAR"
—John B. Archer (arr.) and Kenneth Quivey (music)

I hear a cheer ringing loud and clear,

It brings me back to town;

It comes from men who are shouting again

The name of dear old Brown;

See how they tear through the line,

That raging Brown Bear varsity;

You can bet all you got

That we're taking a shot

At another big victory.

Plunge through that hole!

Give us a goal!

Let's go, Brown Bear, let's go, wow!

Brown Bear, we hear you growling,
Go at them now and bite and scratch and hug!
In all your victories, we'll be rejoicing,
And in defeat we'll still be backing you the same as ever;
In after years the yearning, to be returning,
Just to boost that Bruno series gets us going,
Our hearts o'erflowing
To cheer once more as before for dear old Brown!

We'll always love you, our Alma Mater,
Tenderly and true;
You are our pride, we'll be close by your side
In whatever you may do;
And when our days here are o'er
And we are scattered far away,
You be sure we shall feel
Your most tender appeal,
And we'll come back to you and say;
Plough through that line!
Touchdown this time!
Let's go, Brown Bear, Let's go, Wow!

— — —

"BRING THE VICTORY TO BROWN"
—Donald Jackson, 1909
("Brown" chanted in the background on downbeats throughout the introductory verse)
When John Nich'las Brown arrived here in town,
He says to himself, says he: (what's he say, gov'na?)
"Our college, I vow, I'm going to endow,
To be sure it is named for me." (By jove!)
When years pass along, in prose or in song,
Its fame will ring each day,
With a loud, snappy cheer or a song, ringing clear
This is what they're going to say:

Keep a-cheering for Brunonia!
And her mighty team today;

Stand behind the boys who fight for you!
Ev'ry man must back the play;
Bend your might to win the fight
And beat the vanquished down;
So give a cheer, cheer, cheer for Bruno's team,
And bring the vict'ry home,
And bring the vict'ry home,
And bring the vict'ry home to Brown!

ORIGINAL CHORUS as written in 1919:
Keep a cheering for Brunonia
For we're here to win the day;
Stand behind the boys that fight for you
Every Brown man's in the fray;
Then do your might to win the fight
Our foemen must go down;
So, come on, cheer, cheer, cheer, Brunonia!
And bring the victory to Brown.[207]

— — —

"Brown Victory March"
—William H. McMasters (words) and Edward W. Corliss, 1895 (music)
We're in the game for all it's worth, we're out to win today;
Our men are men of goodly girth, they make a grand array.
They fight for ev'ry inch of ground, they fear no foeman's frown;
They're out to fight, with main and might, for victory and Brown.

Onward we're marching, marching along. For dear old Brown;
Up then and cheer, boys, hearty and strong, for dear old Brown.
For her the honor, for us the work, ever shall be;
Onward and forward, never we'll shirk, marching onto victory.

We love to see her colors wave, when victory is won;
Her prowess, in the field, to save brings out each sturdy son.
To do their best for "Auld Lang Syne," for honor and renown;
They're out today, and in the fray, for victory and Brown.

— — —

"On the Chapel Steps"
—Joel Nelson Eno, Arthur Thomas and Caspar G. Dickson, 1883 (words),
and George Coleman Gow, 1884 (music)
Here at the pleasant twilight hour,
When daily tasks are o'er,
We gather on the chapel steps
To sing our songs once more.
The braided branches of the elms
In silence bend to hear,
And hoary walls and ancient halls
Ring back our tones of cheer.

From ev'ry haunted niche a voice,
That sang in other days
The current of its hopes and joys
Runs softly neath our lays.
Oh, student songs, no mimic arts
Your in-born charms can gain
Ye cheer out thirsty, dusty hearts
Like chiming drops of rain!

When far away in future days
Life's surfeit on us palls;
When vigils cease and turmoil stays,
These ivy mantled walls
From every softly waving leaf
Will send some soothing strain
To lure us gently from our grief,
And give us heart again!

And so, tho' far from college halls
We sing our songs once more;
To cheer our hearts with mem'ries fond
Of days that are of yore,
Those days and years with pleasure bright
Passed by on pinions fleet
But left behind them in their flight
Our friendships oh! How sweet.

— — —

"BRUNONIA/AS WE GO MARCHING"
—Alfred G. Chaffee 1902
As we go marching onward toward the goal,
We always cheer our team with heart and soul;
It's not our wealth that's won us fame,
But it's the way we play the game.
For what we do, we do up Brown! (Brown! Brown!)
Of all the colleges from east to west,
There is but one of all that we love the best,
Tho' her teams may meet defeat,
There's a thing you'll never beat,
It's the loyalty of Sons of Brown! So…

Come on, ye faithful sons of Brown and White,
Get in the game and play with all your might,
Hearts beating fast, will be true till the last
To the men who defend the name of Dear Old Brown!

Chic-Chic Brunonia! Chic-Chic Brunonia!
Brown! Brown! Brown! Brown! B-R-O-W-N Brown! Brown!

— — —

"BRUNO"
—Alfred G. Chaffee, 1902
In peace or war, it's Brunonia, Brunonia, Brunonia
That's what we fight for, Brunonia, Brunonia, for Brown.
With your fair name, dear Brunonia, Brunonia, Brunonia
We'll win the game for Brunonia, Brunonia, for Brown…

With colors flying, every man will be trying
To help Bruno, Bruno, YOU KNOW BRUNO.
He's just a bear, but let me tell you Beware!
Look out for Bruno, Bruno, for Bruno's for Brown.
Brown! Brown! Brown! Brown! Brown! Brown! Brown! Brown!
(repeat)

NOTES

Acknowledgements

1. Though, apparently, there was talk of one being attempted back in 1969. See a letter to the editor by Earl Holt '67, *Brown Alumni Monthly* 70, no. 3 (December 1969): 7.

Chapter 1

2. Martha Mitchell, *Encyclopedia Brunoniana* (Providence, RI: Brown University Library, 1993), 400.
3. Ibid., 401.
4. Biographical File for Arthur Hutchins Colby, Brown University Archives, 1-S.
5. "Brown's First Brass Band," *Providence Journal*, October 27, 1929.
6. "The Brass Band," *Brown Daily Herald*, October 7, 1892, 1.
7. Letter to the Editor, *Brown Daily Herald*, May 10, 1901; Letter to the Editor, *Brown Daily Herald*, April 11, 1902.
8. "Asks Support for Band," *Providence Journal*, March 11, 1916; Mitchell, *Encyclopedia Brunoniana*, 403; "Predecessor Bands," *Brown Alumni Monthly* 65, no. 3 (December 1964): 79.
9. Henry S. Burrage, *Brown University in the Civil War* (Providence, RI: Providence Press Company, 1868), 350; "Author of 'Alma Mater,'" *Providence Journal*, October 23, 1904.

10. "Author of 'Alma Mater,'" *Providence Journal*.

11. Robert Perkins Brown, et al, ed., *Memories of Brown* (Providence, RI: Brown Alumni Monthly, 1909), 186.

12. "Directory of Deceased American Physicians, 1804–1929" Ancestry. com.

13. William Whitman Bailey, "The Author of Alma Mater," *Providence Bulletin*, January 4, 1909, clipped and found in Biographical File for James Andrews DeWolf, Brown University Archives, 1-S.

14. Obituary notice for George Coleman Gow, *Brown Alumni Monthly* 38, no. 7 (February 1938): 205. For other colleges' use of the song, see for example William P. Bigelow, ed., *Amherst College Songs* (Amherst, 1926), *Tufts Songs Nineteen-Fifteen* (Tufts College, 1915) and Thomas N. Robbins, ed., *Songs of Penn State* (New York: Hinds, Noble & Eldredge, 1914).

15. Obituary notice for Joel Nelson Eno, *Brown Alumni Monthly* 37, no. 9 (April 1937): 262.

16. Mitchell, *Encyclopedia Brunoniana*, 508; "In the Mailbox," *Brown Alumni Monthly* 46, no. 7 (May 1946): 162.

17. "Musical Clubs Make Plans for the Year," *Brown Daily Herald*, January 14, 1919, 1.

18. Quivey was Purdue class of 1917. "Pep Session, Fowler Hall, Friday, Nov 24th," n.d., housed in Helen Gould Collection of Purdue Dance Cards and Theater Programs, MSA 294, Box 2, Folder 11, Purdue University Archives.

19. "T. Brown's' Commencement March," *Brown Alumni Monthly* 8, no. 5 (December 1907): 106–7.

20. Arlan R. Coolidge, "How Rhode Island Nearly Lost Reeves and the American Band," *Rhode Island History* 22, no. 2 (April 1963): 37; "At More Than 100 Commencements," *Brown Alumni Monthly* 51, no. 1 (Summer 1950): 18.

21. "T. Brown's Commencement March."

22. "At More Than 100 Commencements"; Mitchell, *Encyclopedia Brunoniana*, 19.

23. Margaret Bingham Stillwell, *The Pageant of Benefit Street Down Through the Years* (Providence, RI: Akerman-Standard Press, 1945), 36.

24. "T. Brown's Commencement March."

25. "The New Brown Song," ad from *Brown Daily Herald*, November 20, 1909, 3; W.T. Hastings, ed., *Songs of Brown University* (Providence, RI, 1921), 42.

26. "Mass Meeting Tonight," *Brown Daily Herald*, November 10, 1905, 1.

27. Notice in *Brown Daily Herald*, October 19, 1912, 4.

28. "Alumnus Writes New Brown Cheering Song," *Brown Daily Herald*, October 24, 1919, 1–2.

29. "Brown Songs," *Brown Daily Herald*, October 20, 1926, 2.

30. Form letter for alumni from Henry S. Chafee, August 24, 1950, found in Donald Jackson biographical file, Brown University Archives, 1-S.

31. "Winning Songs," *Brown Alumni Monthly* 49, no. 1 (July 1948): 13.

32. Class Notices—1895, *Brown Alumni Monthly* 17, no. 3 (October 1916): 82. (Announces the death of Corliss of pneumonia on September 20.)

33. "Alfred G. Chaffee Dies; Attorney and Politician," *Providence Journal*, May 3, 1961, clipping found in Biographical File for Chaffee, Brown University Archives, 1-S.

34. Frances P. O'Connor, ed., *Songs of the Women's College in Brown University* (Providence, RI: The Editor, 1917), 3.

Chapter 2

35. Irving Harris, "Notes on the Early History of the Brown University Band," in Brown University Band Papers, Brown University Archives, OF-1Q-B2.

36. Philip G. Bronstein to W.C. Worthington, 1951.3.14, in University Archives Topic Files, 1-Q Brown Band, writes: "When I transferred to Brown as a sophomore in 1923 I organized the present Brown Band.... Since I was working my way thru as a professional musician I was forced to resign at this time [football season, 1924] and was replaced by Irving Harris."; *Liber Brunensis* 1924, 235.

37. "Candidates for Band Report to Bronstein," *Brown Daily Herald*, October 1, 1924.

38. "Brown Band Begins Season To-Morrow," *Brown Daily Herald*, October 2, 1924.

39. Harris, "Notes," 1.

40. Samuel J. Berard, "The Brown University Band: A Brief History," in Brown University Band Records, Box 13.

41. Harris, "Notes," 3.

42. Ibid., 2. See also *Brown Daily Herald* articles calling rehearsals.

43. Joseph L. Strauss Jr., "Notes on the Early History of the Brown University Band," in Band Records, OF-1Q-B2, 3.

44. Nelson Lambert (1885–1962) was janitor in Faunce House from 1909 to 1952. See Mitchell, *Encyclopedia Brunoniana*, 155.

45. Harris, "Notes," 2.

46. "Big Rally Will Feature Football Practice To-Day," *Brown Daily Herald*, October 8, 1924.

47. "University Band Holds Rehearsal for Parades," *Brown Daily Herald*, October 8, 1924.

48. "Two Hundred Students Follow Band in Rally," *Brown Daily Herald*, October 9, 1924.

49. Strauss, "Notes," 4.

50. Harris, "Notes," 2; *The Harvard Song Book* (2nd ed; Cambridge, MA: Harvard Glee Club, 1923). "Our Director" is one of the pieces of music found in OF-1Q-B2, Box 21.

51. Harris, "Notes," 2.

52. "The Brown Band," *Brown Daily Herald*, November 10, 1924.

53. Otis E. Randall to Irving Harris, November 10, 1924, in Irving Harris scrapbook #1, OF-1Q-B2.

54. "Reorganization of Brown Band Tonight in Union," *Brown Daily Herald*, November 12, 1924.

55. Ibid.

56. What is odd about Manchester is that he was a violist, so it's difficult to know which instrument he played in the band or if he just served as its manager without performing. He continued serving the orchestra in a leadership role.

57. Brown Band Financial Ledger, housed in OF-1Q-B2.

58. Harris, "Notes," 3; "Band Will Appear at Cub Championships as Part of Extensive Spring Program," *Brown Daily Herald*, March 24, 1925.

59. Rehearsal notice, *Brown Daily Herald*, December 15, 1924; "Band Will Appear at Cub Championships."

60. Financial Ledger, OF-1Q-B2; "University Band Has Room for More Men," *Brown Daily Herald*, March 2, 1925.

61. "Open Letter from Cammarian Club," *Brown Daily Herald*, March 21, 1925.

62. Harris, "Notes," 3. The uniforms were purchased by Abraham Harris, Irving's father.

63. Financial Ledger, OF-1Q-B2.

64. Rehearsal notice, *Brown Daily Herald*, April 18, 1925; "Brown University Band Which Will Help Put 'Pep' into the Brunonian Games This Season," *Providence Journal*, April 20, 1925 (pictorial).

65. "Harris Builds a Band at Brown," *Jacobs' Band Monthly*, July 1925, in Irving Harris Scrapbook, vol. 1, OF-1Q-B2; "Brown Turns Tables on Dartmouth," *Brown Daily Herald*, May 18, 1925.

66. "New Sweaters Bought for University Band," *Brown Daily Herald*, October 1, 1925, 1.

67. Harris, "Notes," 4; "Largest Bass Drum in New England Displayed Today," *Brown Daily Herald*, September 26, 1925, 1.

68. "New Sweaters Bought for University Band."

69. Ibid.

70. "Capacity Crowd of Twenty-Seven Thousand Spectators Watch Great Yale Team Overcome Early Brown Lead, Roll Up Three Touchdowns, and Triumph 20–7 at Dedication Game in Stadium," *Brown Daily Herald*, October 26, 1925, 1.

71. Joseph L. Strauss Jr. "Birthday for the Band," *Brown Alumni Monthly* 65, no. 1 (October 1964): 19.

72. "Capacity Crowd of Twenty-Seven Thousand Spectators Watch Great Yale Team Overcome Early Brown Lead."

73. "Brown University Band Makes Great Strides in Year of Life," *Providence Journal*, November 15, 1925.

74. "Local Alumni Plan Formal Concert and Dance at the Biltmore in Early March," *Brown Daily Herald*, January 7, 1926, 1.

75. "Professor S. J. Berard Chosen Band Adviser," *Brown Daily Herald*, March 6, 1926, 1.

76. Harris to Faunce, June 22, 1926, in OF-1Q-B2, Box 4.

77. Banquet program, found pasted in Samuel J. Berard's "Historical Record" of the band, OF-1Q-B2, Box 13.

78. "Biltmore Banquet to Mark End of Successful Season for University Bandsmen," *Brown Daily Herald*, May 17, 1926, 1–4.

79. Ibid.

80. Sometimes mistakenly noted as a trip to Princeton; see *Liber Brunensis* 1928, 226.

81. "Brown Song Records to Be Issued Soon," *Brown Daily Herald*, October 11, 1927, 1.

82. Raymond F. Lynch '42 notes that his father, an RCA distributor, ordered a special pressing of 250 copies and that the records were sold at the music shop on the corner of Thayer and Angell Streets. See Charlotte Bruce Harvey, "Camden Songs: What Did the Brown Band Sound Like in 1927?" *Brown Alumni Magazine*, May/June 2014.

83. *Liber Brunensis* 1928, 53.

84. "400 at Concert by Brown Band," *Providence Journal*, March 27, 1926.

Chapter 3

85. Death Return, City of Providence, for William Herbert Perry Faunce, Certificate #336, Providence City Archives.

86. See Harris's scrapbook #1, OF-1Q-B2.

87. *Liber Brunensis* 1932, 224.

88. "John O. Prouty Wins Harris Band Trophy," *Providence Journal*, June 16, 1930.

89. Ibid.

90. "Brown Band Cup Is Given to Two," *Providence Journal*, February 17, 1935.

91. "Band, Glee Clubs Will Give Fourth Terrace Concert," *Brown Daily Herald*, August 18, 1942, 1.

92. *Liber Brunensis* 1944, 47, notes "Camp Washington." I have been unable to find any place in Rhode Island by this name.

93. "She's Bringing a Friend!" *Brown Daily Herald*, November 19, 1941, 1.

94. "Brown Band Plans to Hold Concerts," *Brown Herald Record*, March 17, 1944, 5; *Liber Brunensis* 1944, 47.

95. *Liber Brunensis* 1944, 47.

96. Biographical File for Everett M. Seixas, Brown University Archives.

97. "Thomas B. Gall, Bandsman, Dead," *Providence Journal*, September 10, 1938; "The Coach of the Band," *Brown Alumni Monthly*, November 1938, 121.

98. "Jovite Labonte Named to Coach Bandsmen at Brown University," *Providence Journal*, February 8, 1939; Berard to Thomas W. Taylor, February 1, 1939, OF-1Q-B2, Box 4.

99. "Edward A. Denish, Leader of Well-Known Bands, Dies," *Providence Journal*, August 9, 1961.

100. A series of summer concerts is mentioned in a letter from Edward A. Denish to Samuel J. Berard, July 2, 1942, OF-1Q-B2, Box 4.

101. Rose helped advise department chair Arlan Coolidge on hiring Fischer. See letter from Coolidge to Rose, March 22, 1947, Brown University Department of Music Records, OF-1ZMU-1, Box 6.

102. The new uniforms were purchased for the Princeton game on October 4, 1947; see "New Uniforms Appear Sat.," *Brown Daily Herald*, October 1, 1947, 1-2.

103. *Liber Brunensis* 1948.

104. "Iacuele's Gamesness Inspires Team; Brown Band Enlivens Spectacle," *Brown Daily Herald*, October 18, 1948, 3.

105. Chester V. Cheek to Arlan R. Coolidge, May 25, 1948, OF-1ZMU-1, Box 7.

106. Martin J. Fischer to Leroy Anderson, November 3, 1947; Anderson to Fischer, November 12, 1947; Fischer to Anderson, January 24, 1948; Anderson to Fischer, April 5, 1948. All present in OF-1ZMU-1, Box 7.

107. Cheek to Coolidge, May 25, 1948, OF-1ZMU-1, Box 7.

108. Martin Fischer to Fred A. Otis, October 1, 1948, OF-1ZMU-1, Box 8.

109. Notice in the *Brown Daily Herald*, December 13, 1948.

110. "Brown Band Adopts Flexible Constitution; Articles Aid Morale," *Brown Daily Herald*, March 17, 1949, 1–2.

111. Though Columbia claims to be the first school to institute the style in the early 1950s, Harvard claims it introduced the style circa 1946.

112. Neil Donovan, "Big Brown Team Tops the Cross," *Brown Daily Herald*, November 3, 1947, 5.

113. *Liber Brunensis* 1955, 105.

114. *Liber Brunensis* 1950.

115. "Harris Band Trophy Given to Jim James," *Brown Daily Herald*, December 17, 1957, 1–2.

116. Personal interview with Farrell Fleming '62.

117. Script @ Harvard, November 12, 1955, found in OF-1Q-B2, Box 16.

118. Interviews with alumni Ulysses S. James '58 and Michael Weston '60.

119. "Band Stunts for 1956 Football Season," OF-1Q-B2, Box 16.

120. "Harris Band Trophy Given to Jim James," *Brown Daily Herald*, December 17, 1957, 1–2.

121. Washington Metropolitan Philharmonic Association, www.wmpamusic.org.

122. Script vs. URI, October 25, 1958, OF-1Q-B2, Box 16.

123. Script @ Harvard, November 15, 1958, OF-1Q-B2, Box 16.

124. Script vs Harvard, November 14, 1959, OF-1Q-B2, Box 16.

Chapter 4

125. John C. McWilliams, *The 1960s Cultural Revolution* (Westport, CT: Greenwood Press, 2000), 84.

126. Ibid.

127. M. Charles Bakst, "Brown Band Revises Show Under Pressure," *Brown Daily Herald*, October 7, 1963, 1–2.

128. Script vs. Penn, October 1, 1966, OF-1Q-B2, Box 16.

129. Script vs. Colgate, October 23, 1965, OF-1Q-B2, Box 16.

130. Ibid.

131. "Speaks Up for Brown's Band," *Evening Bulletin* clipping, circa 1964, found in Harris scrapbook #1, OF-1Q-B2.

132. Script @ Columbia, November 23, 1968, OF-1Q-B2, Box 16.

133. Script @ Columbia, November 21, 1970, OF-1Q-B2, Box 16.

134. Photographs and captions by Stuart Crump in *Brown Alumni Monthly* 66, no. 2 (November 1965): 31, 37.

135. "Frank Marinaccio—Musician," *Providence Journal*, February 20, 1966.

136. Script @ Cornell, November 11, 1967, OF-1Q-B2, Box 16.

137. David M. Evans to the Brown University Marching Band, November 14, 1967, in Ray Lorenzo Heffner Papers, OF-1C-13, Box 28, University Archives.

138. "Open Letter," *Brown Daily Herald*, November 14, 1967, 2.

139. Script vs. UPenn, October 5, 1968.

140. "Band 'E' Formation Arouses GOP Ire," *Brown Daily Herald*, November 9, 1964, 1.

141. J.E. Tribble to Ray L. Heffner, October 11, 1968, Heffner Papers, Box 3.

142. Herman M. Harris to unknown recipient, October 29, 1969, OF-1Q-B2, Box 8.

143. "Brown University Orchestra: History," www.brown.edu/Departments/Music/sites/orchestra/history.

144. Laurence Pizer to Barbara Jeremiah, November 6, 1971, OF-1Q-B2, Box 8.

145. Band Board Minutes, March 16, 1969, OF-1Q-B2, Box 4.

146. Ibid.

147. "Women Given Full Equality in Brown's Marching Band," *Providence Journal*, March 17, 1969.

148. Script vs. Yale, October 11, 1969.

149. Script vs. Harvard, November 15, 1969.

150. John Roberti, "Mascot Continues Quest for Presidency," *Brown Daily Herald*, April 18, 1988, 1; "For Immediate Release" (press release from Snidley's campaign), Brown Band Personal Archive Collection.

Chapter 5

151. Jeremy Schlosberg, "Skating Tooters," *Brown Daily Herald*, February 6, 1978, 1–2.

152. "Ladies Night at Brown-B.C. Hockey Game Tonight," *Brown Daily Herald*, January 18, 1934, 1.

153. Recent performances can be found on YouTube by Ohio State University (www.youtube.com/watch?v=PuY3LWQlCrg) and Boston University (www.youtube.com/watch?v=foyxJFAgW-A).

154. "Brown University Band on Skates," video clip RHiX_1986.93.20290, WJAR Archives, Rhode Island Historical Society.

155. *Brown Daily Herald*, February 17, 1970.

156. *Boston Globe*, December 16, 1977.

157. Ray Fitzgerald, "He Strikes Up Brown's Band," *Boston Globe*, November 7, 1978.

158. *Liber Brunensis* 1959.

159. Kathleen Colgan, "The Foxboro Four and the Harvard Drum," *Brown Alumni Monthly* 74 no. 4 (January 1974): 56.

160. "Band's Big Bass Drum Stolen; Five [*sic*] Brown Students Arrested," *Harvard Crimson*, November 16, 1973.

161. Colgan, "Foxboro Four and the Harvard Drum."

162. "Respectability in Football," *Brown Alumni Monthly* 74 no. 5 (February 1974): 46.

163. Michael Silverstein, "Judge Dismisses Foxboro Four Case; Gives 'No Sentence, No Record, No Fine,'" *Brown Daily Herald*, December 11, 1973, 1–2.

164. Mitchell, *Encyclopedia Brunoniana*, 524.

165. "Band Records," *Brown Daily Herald*, May 10, 1974, 3.

166. Phil Sunshine, "Harvard Drum Heist Foiled; Band Halftime Show Censored," *Brown Daily Herald*, November 16, 1973, 1–6.

167. "Halftime Shows Are Censored," *Providence Journal*, October 9, 1974.

168. Script vs. Yale, October 11, 1975, OF-1Q-B2, Box 16.

169. Script vs. Harvard, November 4, 1978, OF-1Q-B2, Box 16.

170. Jonathan Karp, "Striking Up Controversy," *Brown Daily Herald*, September 29, 1982, 1–4.

171. Script @ West Point, September 26, 1981, OF-1Q-B2, Box 16.

172. Ibid.

173. "Strike Out the Band," *Sports Illustrated*, October 12, 1981, OF-1Q-B2, Box 19.

174. Robert A. Reichley to Walter (?), October 6, 1981, OF-1Q-B2, Box 8.

175. B. Franklin Reinauer to Howard R. Swearer, September 28, 1981, OF-1Q-B2, Box 8.

176. Rafael Jorge Garcia to Howard R. Swearer, September 29, 1981, OF-1Q-B2, Box 8.

177. Gregory A. Voigt, "Letter to the Editor," *Brown Daily Herald*, October 5, 1981.

178. Warren St. John, "And the Band Misbehaved On…," *New York Times*, September 29, 2002.

179. Steve Mufson, "Ivy League Bands Keep on Marching to X-Rated Tunes," *Wall Street Journal*, September 25, 1981. OF-1Q-B2, Box 19.

180. *The University of Pennsylvania Band* (Charleston, SC: Arcadia Publishing, 2006), 109.

181. IBC Constitution, Brown Band Personal Collection.

182. Script @ Holy Cross, October 24, 1981, OF-1Q-B2, Box 16.

183. Steve Volling, "Maestro McGarrell to Direct Bruin Band," *Brown Daily Herald*, September 21, 1984, 1–5.

184. Script vs. Penn, October 13, 1984.

185. Andrew Skoler, "Today Show Gets Ready for Breakfast at Brown," *Brown Daily Herald*, October 16, 1985, 1–9.

186. David Fedor, "Brown Band Cuts Album, for Fun and Profit," *Brown Daily Herald*, October 23, 1987, 7.

187. Ibid.

188. David Lee Strasburg, "Band Bursts into 65th Year," *Brown Daily Herald*, September 27, 1988, 3.

189. Tim Vandenack, "I Want My BTV," *Brown Daily Herald*, October 24, 1986, 6.

190. Image and caption in *Brown Daily Herald*, October 3, 1988, 10.

191. "Orange Bomb," *Brown Daily Herald*, October 31, 1988, 2.

192. Steven Perelman, "Pumpkin Pounds Sayles Pavement," *Brown Daily Herald*, November 1, 1988, 1.

193. Ian Reifowitz, "So Close!" *Brown Daily Herald*, October 7, 1991, 7.

194. Lee Drutman, "Arts, Culture, Politics, and Marinara Sauce," *Brown Daily Herald*, November 7, 1997, 13.

Chapter 6

195. Jessika Sorrosa, "Band Battles Censors," *Brown Daily Herald*, October 21, 1991, 1, 3.

196. Diana Henschke, "Brown Band Unites Music, Mayhem," *Brown Daily Herald*, September 11, 1997, 1.

197. Katherine Blank, "Oral History as a Sacred Ritual," course paper for AMCV1611, Brown Band personal collection, 2.

198. Ira Berkow, "A Button for All Occasions—Including Brown vs. Harvard," *New York Times*, September 28, 2002, D1, D5.

199. Traditions of the Band," audio cassette housed in OF-1Q-B2.

200. Simon Bronner, *Campus Traditions: Folklore from the Old-Time College to the Modern Mega-University* (Jackson: University Press of Mississippi, 2012), xiii.

201. Script vs. Princeton, October 18, 2014.

202. The Brown Band, "Scripts," brownband.org/scripts/fall-2017.

203. Brown University Athletics, brownbears.com/sports/football/schedule/2017.

204. Script vs. Cornell, February 14, 2020, brownband.org/scripts/spring-2020.

Appendix

205. William Albion Hart, "Brown Ki-Yi-Yi March," Harris Collection of American Poetry and Plays, John Hay Library, HB26448 RI.

206. Alternatively, the names of presidents in place of Prexy, i.e. Wriston, Keeney, Paxson.

207. "Alumnus Writes New Brown Cheering Song," *Brown Daily Herald*, October 24, 1919, 1.

BIBLIOGRAPHY

Manuscripts
(all from Brown University Archives unless otherwise stated)

Brown University Archives Biographical Files, 1-S. Collection of files containing news clippings, photographs and letters related to Brown University Alumni. Compiled by the Alumni office in the twentieth century and then transferred to the library archives.

Brown University Band Personal Archives, 1924–present. A collection of papers maintained by the band historians, most of which are duplicates of material in the University Archives.

Brown University Band Records, 1924–2017 (1959–2004), OF-1Q-B2 (21 boxes). The official records of the band, containing twenty-one boxes, one cassette tape, a collection of buttons, three scrapbooks, the Harris Trophy and Irving Harris's band sweater.

Brown University Department of Music Records, OF-1ZMU-1 (39 boxes).

Classified Topic Files, Band, 1-Q (1 box). News clippings, letters, etc. related to the band, kept by the university archivist.

Helen Gould Collection of Purdue Dance Cards and Theater Programs, Purdue University Archives.

Howard Robert Swearer Papers, 1976–90 (1977–78), OF-1C-15 (128 boxes).

Ray Lorenzo Heffner Papers, 1966–69, OF-1C-13 (41 boxes).

University Archives Photograph Collection.

WJAR Video Archives, Rhode Island Historical Society.

Books and Articles

Bronner, Simon. *Campus Traditions: Folklore from the Old-Time College to the Modern Mega-University*. Jackson: University Press of Mississippi, 2012.

Brown, Robert Perkins, ed. *Memories of Brown: Traditions and Recollections Gathered from Many Sources*. Providence, RI: Brown Alumni Magazine, 1909.

Burrage, Henry S. *Brown University in the Civil War: A Memorial*. Providence, RI: Providence Press Company, 1868.

Colby, Arthur Hutchins. *Songs of Brown University*. Boston: Silver, Burdett, & Co., 1891.

Coolidge, Arlan R. "How Rhode Island Nearly Lost Reeves and the American Band." *Rhode Island History* 22, no. 2 (April 1963): 33–37.

Hastings, William T., and Thomas B. Appleget, eds. *Songs of Brown University*. Providence, RI: The University, 1921.

McPhee, Ralph W. *Songs of Brown University*. New York: Hinds, Noble and Eldredge, 1908.

McWilliams, John C. *The 1960s Cultural Revolution*. Westport, CT: Greenwood Press, 2000.

Mitchell, Martha. *Encyclopedia Brunoniana*. Providence, RI: Brown University Library, 1993.

O'Connor, Frances P., ed. *Songs of the Women's College in Brown University*. Providence, RI, 1917.

Stillwell, Margaret Bingham. *The Pageant of Benefit Street Down Through the Years*. Providence, RI: Akerman-Standard Press, 1945.

Strauss, Joseph L. "Birthday for the Band." *Brown Alumni Monthly* 65, no. 1 (October 1964): 16–19.

The University of Pennsylvania Band. Charleston, SC: Arcadia Publishing, 2006.

Periodicals and Annual Works

Brown Alumni Monthly (later *Brown Alumni Magazine*)

Brown Daily Herald, 1892–present.

Liber Brunensis, various years between 1915 and 2023.

Providence Journal and *Providence Evening Bulletin*

Miscellaneous articles from the *Boston Globe*, *Harvard Crimson*, *Sports Illustrated* and *Wall Street Journal*, clippings from which are found in the band records (OF-1Q-B2).

Other

American Medical Association. "Directory of Deceased American Physicians, 1804–1929." Ancestry. www.ancestry.com/search/collections/7833.

Brown University Orchestra. "A Brief History." www.brown.edu/Departments/Music/sites/orchestra/about/history.

Personal interviews with various alumni as referenced in the acknowledgements.

Washington Metropolitan Philharmonic Association. www.wmpamusic.org.

ABOUT THE AUTHOR

*S*ean Briody was raised in Commack, Long Island, New York, where he attended Commack High School and graduated with an IB Diploma. Sean started at Brown in the fall of 2015 and quickly joined the Brown Band, which became an integral part of his college experience. He graduated Brown in 2019 with honors and a dual degree in American Studies and Egyptology/Assyriology. He currently lives in Columbia, South Carolina, where he works as a social studies teacher and history bowl coach at Cardinal Newman School. He has also worked for the Brown Library and Providence's historic North Burial Ground. Sean enjoys collecting antique books, coins, and historical memorabilia.

The author in uniform, 2019. *Brown University Band.*